Got Goodness?
Think Again!

We Are Not as Good as We Think We Are
And the Reasons Why

Jay L. Wenger

CHESTER RIVER PRESS
2013

ISBN: 978-0-9833159-8-8

Cover Design by James Dissette

FIRST EDITION

Chester River Press
Chestertown, Maryland
www.chesterriverpress.com

I thank my wife, Susie, and daughter, Kira,
for their unending love, patience, and support.

CONTENTS

Foreword   1

Chapter 1: Exaggerations Abound   3

Chapter 2: More Complex Than We Realize   9

Chapter 3: Do We Really Know What We Believe?   21

Chapter 4: Unconscious Content: It Matters   31

Chapter 5: Love the Sinner? Hate the Sin?   41

Chapter 6: The Illusion of an Open Mind   49

Chapter 7: I Am Right; You Are Wrong   59

Chapter 8: Overvalued Values   71

Chapter 9: The Naïve Notion That "I Could Never Hurt Anyone"   81

Chapter 10: The Do-Gooder's Dilemma   89

Chapter 11: Unconscious Processing: It's Superior   99

Chapter 12: Final Thoughts   111

References and Notes   117

Foreword

Occasionally when people meet me for the first time and find out that I am a psychology professor, they express caution. They know that many psychologists work professionally as therapists, identifying various disorders and recommending possible treatments. They assume I might also try to size them up in some way.

But I am not a clinical or counseling type of psychologist. I am a research psychologist – one who is interested in conducting experiments to find out anything I can about what it means to be human. So I usually tell people they have nothing to worry about. I am not going to analyze them. Recently, however, my daughter has been challenging me: "Dad, you might not be a clinical or counseling psychologist, but you do analyze people." She's right. I am fascinated by human behavior, and I do try to sort through the possibilities for why people say and do the things they do. And that includes my own talk and behavior.

I am particularly intrigued with the way we come to believe in our own goodness, compared to others, and often seem so willing to portray it in some way. Myself included. And I am fascinated in how our beliefs about goodness, who has more of it and who doesn't, is often based on political preferences. For example, we readily assume that those who agree with us politically are somehow better than those who do not. Perhaps we consider those who agree with us to be better informed or somehow more concerned about important issues in life.

I am also intrigued with how we generally assume that we would always do what is good and upright in a difficult situation. Situations are complex, and we are too. There are several studies in psychology suggesting that we rarely step up to the degree we think we would. There are also studies indicating that we are much more complex than we realize. Thus, it should not be surprising that we will always have difficulty in completely understanding ourselves and what we might do in any situation.

Finally, I acknowledge that the title of this book suggests the book will be pessimistic: "We are not as good as we think we are." On the contrary, I believe this book is optimistic and very positive. Re-evaluating our own perceptions of goodness, our own goodness and that of others, is an important first step to becoming more tolerant and better people. Note, too, that I am not suggesting that any one of us is not a good person. I am simply suggesting that very few of us are as good as we think we are.

I hope you find the book interesting and challenging. I describe a variety of studies in psychology, so I hope the book also piques an interest in the contributions of research psychologists.

Chapter 1

Exaggerations Abound

"We are all self-righteous hypocrites."
– Jonathan Haidt, *The Righteous Mind*

You probably heard of the term "inferiority complex." It was coined in the 1940s by a psychologist named Alfred Adler.[1] It is true that we occasionally feel lousy about ourselves, but these moments of feeling inferior tend to be short-lived. Unless we are dealing with a serious mental disorder, we usually get over it rather quickly. So instead of believing we all have an inferiority complex, it is more accurate to say that most of us have something like a "superiority complex."[2] And it seems particularly true when we are thinking about our own goodness. The evidence is overwhelming!

I will start with those who are younger. In an extensive survey as part of college entrance examinations, over 800,000 high school students in the United States were asked to compare themselves with others their own age, on several skills or qualities. When it came to evaluating how well they could get along with others – a staple in being considered a good person – virtually all participants reported they were above average. Furthermore, 60% reported they were among the super good, the top 10%, and 25% reported that they were among the top 1%.[3]

Those who are older among us are not immune to similar exaggerations. In a study conducted in Connecticut, researchers tapped into over 800 participants from the general population using a random sampling technique.[4] Participants' average age was around 40 years. Using phone interviews, participants were asked to evaluate their perceived concern for various social issues compared to others in the general population. The issues included concern for the environment, concern for those in society who are homeless, and concern for the poor and hungry in the world – more staples in being considered a good person.

The interviews were conducted in a way so participants could know for sure that their responses would be anonymous and confidential. Nonetheless, participants tended to exaggerate their concern for the environment, for those who are homeless, and for people around the world who are hungry. Specifically 66% of the participants reported that they were appropriately concerned or overly concerned about these issues. But when they evaluated others in the general public, they thought only 32% were similarly concerned. A high majority of these participants acknowledged that they do not do very much to help improve anything related to these issues or concerns, like volunteering time or contributing money. The upshot seems to be "we do not do much to help, but we sure do care."

And our perceptions of goodness are sure to be rewarded. Paradise probably awaits. According to one study, many of us are very confident that someday we will be rewarded with heavenly bliss, as summed up by David Myers:

> What happens when we die? Asked by *U.S. News and World Report* who was at least "somewhat likely" to go to heaven, 19 percent of Americans thought that O.J. Simpson was likely to be welcomed at the pearly gates. As of the poll date, 1997, they were more optimistic about Bill Clinton (52%), Princess Diana (60%), and Michael Jordan (65%). The second closest person to a perceived shoo-in was Mother Teresa (79%). And who do you suppose topped Mother Teresa? At the head of the class with 87 percent perceived heavenly admission rate, people placed *themselves*.[5]

It is not enough that we think we are rather angelic in the here-and-now. There is also research to suggest that we believe our goodness will actually increase in the future. In a study conducted in Norway, researchers had one group of participants evaluate themselves compared to other people who were the same age and same sex.[6] They had another group evaluate how they envisioned themselves to be, compared to same-aged and same-sexed others, *two years from now*. The evaluations addressed favorable qualities such as friendliness, intelligence, and dependability. It also included unfavorable qualities such as self-centeredness, irrationality, and laziness.

Participants rated themselves relatively high on favorable qualities and relatively low on unfavorable qualities, compared to others. Not surprising. The difference was that participants tended to believe both they and others would generally improve on these qualities in the near future, with themselves improving the most. So presumably our perceived superiority over others will become even more pronounced in the future.

Such results remind me of Joe Namath, the former great football player who had a reputation for arrogance and flamboyance. His autobiography is entitled, *I Can't Wait Until Tomorrow . . . 'Cause I Get Better-Looking Every Day.*[7] For the rest of us, we can probably proclaim that "we can't wait until tomorrow, because we will be better and even more deserving of heavenly bliss."

But is it possible that we do not actually believe our exaggerated claims that show up in these kinds of studies? Perhaps the exaggerations are simply a matter of trying to impress the researchers, at least for the moment, despite the fact that we know our responses are anonymous. Or, perhaps we are simply trying to give the type of responses that we believe the researchers want. After all, if a study appears to be about goodness, then we should probably do something to promote goodness.

Researchers at Cornell University designed an experiment to evaluate the degree to which participants actually believe their own portrayals of goodness.[8] First, they had participants take a fake personality test that appeared to evaluate several aspects of goodness. After participants completed the bogus test, they asked participants to estimate how well they believed they scored, relative to other participants who had ostensibly taken the same test. Now participants had a chance to report whether they believed they were among the top 50%, top 30%, top 10%, and so on. They could report any percentage between 1 and 100.

Participants were also given the opportunity to make a series of gambles based on their estimations, and they could earn $1.00 for each win, or correct estimation. But each gamble involved a choice. The first choice was to trust that their reported estimate of goodness was accurate. The second choice was to doubt their estimate and to instead, choose to gamble on a random event that was constructed with similar odds. In the first case, participants could earn $1.00 if their score on a given aspect of goodness was as good as, or topped that of another participant who was randomly selected from all other participants. In the second case, participants could randomly select a token from a jar that contained tokens numbered from 1 to 100. They would win and earn the $1.00, if they picked a number that was inferior to the ranking they estimated for their own goodness.

If participants genuinely believed the rankings they gave for their own goodness, then they should consider both of these gambles to have equal probabilities. Thus it would not matter which of the two gambles they chose. This is what happened. First, participants consistently estimated that they were better than average on many aspects of goodness. Second, they were equally willing to have their gambles based on their estimated goodness, relative to others, as they were to have their gambles based on random drawings with the similar odds. This suggests we indeed believe our own portrayals of goodness.

Any Exceptions?

Do our exaggerations of goodness extend to all areas of our lives? Not necessarily. Several studies have indicated that we are much more likely to exaggerate our goodness when it is linked to morality than when it is associated with intellect.[9]

This tendency to exaggerate moral goodness more so than intellectual prowess is affectionately termed "The Muhammad Ali Effect," named for the famed heavyweight boxing champion. Muhammad Ali's autobiography is entitled *The Greatest: My Own Story*.[10] Ali considered himself to be the greatest in many ways, a superiority complex indeed. When it came to boxing, he was. However, when he failed a reading and writing exam administered by the U.S. military in 1964, Ali backed off and admitted, "I only said I was the greatest, not the smartest."[11]

But why is it that we readily exaggerate our moral goodness, yet we are careful about exaggerating our intellectual goodness? There are two reasons. First, it is likely that moral goodness is more highly favored than intellectual goodness, and according to some researchers, it's likely that this occurs in all cultures.[12] As a result, we are much more motivated to see ourselves as morally top-notch, compared to being smart. Second, moral goodness is probably more subjective and harder to evaluate that intellectual goodness. Thus, it is easier for us to get away with exaggerating moral goodness compared to intellectual prowess.

Many of us have taken IQ tests when we were young. If not, we certainly received academic-related feedback about how smart we were in school. That kind of feedback indicated something about intellect. So we have a history of receiving fairly objective information about how smart we are compared to others. It is unlikely, however, that we ever received similar objective feedback about moral goodness. So it is easier for us to convince ourselves about our compassion, kindness, generosity, et cetera, compared to our intellectual prowess.[13] As the saying goes, "If you open your mouth and speak-up, you are likely to remove all doubt about how smart you are." But if you open your mouth and speak-up about your moral concern for this-and-that, people might actually believe you.

In Sum

Somewhere along the line, many of us have been exposed to teachings that suggest we should be very careful about envisioning ourselves as overly good and better than others. And certainly we should be careful about promoting it. Buddha emphasized it: "It is easy to see the faults of others, but difficult to see one's own faults." And Jesus said, "Why do you see the speck in your neighbor's eye, but do not notice the log in your own eye? . . . You hypocrite, first take the log out of your own eye, and then you will see clearly."[14]

Nonetheless, we go on envisioning ourselves in overly favorable ways. As Myers describes,

> We remember and justify our past actions in self-enhancing ways.
> We exhibit an inflated confidence in the accuracy of our beliefs and judgments.
> We overestimate how desirably we would act in situations where most people behave less than admirably.
> We often seek out favorable, self-enhancing information.
> We are quicker to believe flattering descriptions of ourselves than unflattering ones, and we are impressed

with psychological tests that make us look good.
We exhibit group pride – a tendency to see our group (our
school, our country, our race) as superior.[15]

And did I mention that 94% of college professors believe they are better workers than the average colleague.[16] Count me among the 94%. Most
likely we also believe we have more concern for the environment, more concern for those in society who are homeless, and more concern for the poor
and hungry in the world.

But we too have fallen prey to self-serving tendencies. Leonard Mlodinow suggests that many of us, the so-called experts in human behavior,
haven't been as smart as we think, at least when it comes to understanding
"how we understand ourselves." He says,

> For many decades, research psychologists thought of people
> [including themselves] as detached observers who access
> events and then apply reason to discover truth and decipher
> the nature of the social world. We were said to gather data
> on ourselves and to build our self-images based on gener-
> ally good and accurate inferences. In that traditional view, a
> well-adjusted person was thought to be like a scientist of the
> self, whereas an individual whose self-image was clouded
> by illusion was regarded as vulnerable to, if not already a
> victim of, mental illness. Today, we know the opposite is
> closer to the truth. Normal and healthy individuals – stu-
> dents, professors, engineers, lieutenant colonels, doctors,
> business executives – tend to think of themselves as not
> just competent but proficient [and superior], even if they
> aren't.[17]

Chapter 2

More Complex Than We Realize

"We must give up the insane illusion that the conscious self,
however virtuous and however intelligent,
can do its work singlehanded and without assistance."
– Aldous Huxley, *The Education of an Amphibian*

Benjamin Franklin once stated that "there are three things extremely hard – steel, a diamond, and to know one's self."[1] Good point. However, when it comes to knowing one's self, this is an understatement. Franklin should have added that it is more than difficult. Given the complexity of the human mind, it is impossible to completely know one's self.

The human mind is extremely complex. It processes information at two levels of awareness – one conscious and one unconscious. What goes on consciously is easier to identify and understand. Thus, we generally assume this is the only level that dictates what we do and what we believe. But it is not that simple. Many researchers have demonstrated that what goes on unconsciously is much more important than we realize, and in many ways, that's the crux for why we cannot completely know ourselves and why we have such difficulty evaluating ourselves accurately, in comparison to others.

Theories that describe what goes on consciously and unconsciously are termed dual-process theories.[2] Processes that occur at the conscious level of awareness tend to require effort – mental work. At this level, it seems that we exert voluntary control over our thoughts, and you might say it actually feels like we are thinking. Such processing is good, because it allows us to make careful decisions about important matters in life. The downside is that we cannot easily focus on more than one thought at a time. As a result, many researchers propose that conscious processing consumes mental resources that are limited in nature. The more resources we use to focus on one thought, the fewer we will have available for a second thought.

Processes that occur at the unconscious level seem to occur without much, if any, mental effort. As a result they are usually considered to be automatic in nature. This is good, because it allows us to deal with much more information at any given time. For an example, consider a basketball player. As the player practices dribbling a basketball, he or she will be able to do it by relying mostly on unconscious processing. This allows the player to allocate more conscious processing to monitor the movements of teammates and defensive players. The downside for unconscious processing is that if something unexpected happens, then the automatic nature of what goes on unconsciously might not be best.

Figure 2.1 presents a picture of the human mind with two kinds of activity running through it. Conscious processing is portrayed as one thick and wavy line. It is thick because it's the most noticeable kind of processing in the mind. It is wavy because it's the slowest kind of processing. As noted, it readily consumes resources from some overall allotment. John Bargh and Tonya Chartrand say you can think of it as "heavy processing."[3]

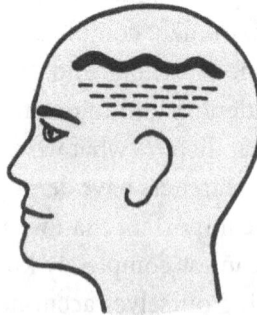

Figure 2.1: Two Levels of Processing

Unconscious processing is portrayed with multiple dashed lines. There are multiple lines because this is the kind of processing that allows us to deal with a lot of information at one time. The lines are dashed because this kind of processing can occur very quickly. Bargh and Chartrand say you can think of it as "light processing."

These two levels of processing always occur simultaneously as we deal with information in our lives. Consider two examples. First, consider what happens when you drive a car and carry on a conversion with a friend at the same time. Many of the requirements for driving a car are well-rehearsed and fairly automatic in nature. Thus, we can save a fair amount of conscious processing for carrying on the conversation. But if the car has manual, stick-shift transmission, and you are a novice with stick-shift, you might need to devote almost all your conscious processing for shifting gears. The conversation will need to wait. Unconscious processes, however, will still help monitor other traffic and pedestrians who are close by, and they will help identify all traffic signals and initiate responses as needed.

For a second example, consider what happens as you read words, sentences, and paragraphs in a book. Several years ago, my daughter asked if I thought it was possible to see words without actually reading them, without interpreting them in some way. My initial answer was "It depends on what you mean by reading." If you mean conscious reading, so you can describe to others what you were reading about, the answer is probably "Yes." But if you mean more automatic and unconscious reading in a way that you cannot easily describe to others what you were reading, the answer is "No."

Then I gave this example. Imagine you are reading a story about a rabbit eagerly hopping about in a garden full of vegetables. But your mind has wandered. So in a sense, you are not thinking about what you are reading. Nonetheless, your mind is being exposed to the information about the rabbit, and you might say you are reading the words unconsciously. Then what would happen if someone were to interrupt you, and ask, "How do you spell the word hair or hare?" Several studies have indicated that you will be more likely to say "h-a-r-e" than if you had not been reading the story about the rabbit. Thus, exposure to the word rabbit, even though it occurred without conscious awareness, sets you up to think rabbit, consciously, when asked to spell hair or hare.

Daniel Kahneman, the Nobel laureate and author of *Thinking, Fast and Slow,* describes the combination of conscious and unconscious processing this way:

> When you are asked what you are thinking about, you can normally answer. You believe you know what goes on in your mind, which often consists of one conscious thought

leading in an orderly way to another. But that is not the only way the mind works, nor indeed is that the typical way. Most impressions and thoughts arise in your conscious experience without your knowing how they got there. You cannot trace how you came to the belief that there is a lamp on the desk in front of you, or how you detected a hint of irritation in [your friend's] voice on the telephone, or how you managed to avoid a threat on the road before you became consciously aware of it. The mental work that produces impressions, intuitions, and many decisions goes on in silence in our mind.[4]

I am guessing that most of us have already been familiar with the concept of unconscious processing and knew that it contributes to human behavior as described above. But I am guessing we have not understood the magnitude of such influence. Anything that we think, feel, or do, is the result of a massive amount of mental activity, and a very high majority of it goes on under the surface of conscious awareness. What we experience consciously is only a small fraction of all that has happened. Sigmund Freud, the champion in promoting the unconscious level of awareness, once suggested that it might be around 86% that goes on unconsciously. Current research suggests it's more like 99%.[5] No wonder we have had such difficulty getting accurate conceptions of ourselves.

And Timothy Wilson, author of *Strangers to Ourselves*, says,

It is true that people have privileged access to a great deal of information about themselves, such as the content of their current thoughts and memories and the object of their attention. But these are mental contents, not mental processes. The real action in the mind is mental processing that produces feelings, judgments, and behaviors. Although we often have access to the results of these processes . . . we do not have access to the mental processes that produced them.

[It is as if unconscious processing] is a pervasive yet hidden engine humming beneath the surface of the mind, and there is no engine hatch that we can open to take a direct look at its operation.[6]

There are several researchers who argue that the distinction between what is conscious and unconscious is not a matter of different "levels" of processing, as Wilson's "hidden engine" analogy suggests. Instead, the distinction is a matter of "stages."[7] In this view, what is unconscious represents the first stage, and what is conscious represents the second stage. It is only during the second stage that conscious awareness occurs.

In this book, however, I will continue to use terminology that suggests the distinction is a matter of levels. Thus, our awareness for what is going on will always be considered as either *below or above* the threshold for conscious awareness, as opposed to being *before or after* the threshold.

The Adaptive Unconscious

Recently, several researchers in psychology have been using the term "adaptive" to describe what goes on unconsciously – hence, the "adaptive unconscious."[8] Think about it. There are two clear adaptive, survival-related advantages that the unconscious level of awareness has over the conscious level. First, it can deal with a lot more information at any given time. Second, its processing can occur much faster.

In a national best-selling book, *Blink: The Power of Thinking Without Thinking,* Malcolm Gladwell describes it this way:

> The study of [the effectiveness of the adaptive unconscious] is one of the most important new fields in psychology. The adaptive unconscious is not to be confused with the unconscious described by Sigmund Freud, which was a dark and murky place filled with desires and memories and fantasies that were too disturbing for us to think about consciously. This new notion of the adaptive unconscious is thought of, instead, as a kind of giant computer that quickly and quietly processes a lot of the data we need in order to keep functioning as human beings. When you walk out into the street and suddenly realize that a truck is bearing down on you, do you have time to think through all your options? Of course not.

The only way that human beings could ever have survived as a species for as long as we have is that we've developed another kind of decision-making apparatus that's capable of making very quick judgments based on very little information.[9]

Thus, what goes on unconsciously should not only be acknowledged. It should be celebrated. It represents a massive set of processes all working for our well-being and benefit. Wilson puts it this way:

Consider that at any given moment, our five senses are taking in more than 11,000,000 pieces of information. Scientists have determined this number by counting the receptor cells each sense organ has and the nerves that go from these cells to the brain. Our eyes alone receive and send over 10,000,000 signals to our brain each second. Scientists have also tried to determine how many of these signals can be processed consciously at any given point in time, by looking at such things as how quickly people can read, consciously detect different flashes of light, and tell apart different kinds of smells. The most liberal estimate is that people can process consciously about 40 pieces of information per second. Think about it: we take in 11,000,000 pieces of information a second, but can process only 40 of them consciously. What happens to the other 10,999,960? It would be terribly wasteful to design a system with such incredible sensory acuity but very little capacity to use the incoming information. Fortunately, we do make use of a great deal of this information outside of conscious awareness.[10]

In Figure 2.1, conscious processing is represented with one thick line and unconscious processing is represented with four dashed lines. But if conscious processing deals with 40 bits of information per second and unconscious processing deals with about 11,000,000 bits, then what goes on unconsciously is about 200,000 times greater in dealing with information than what goes on consciously. Surely there should be many more dashed lines for unconscious processing in that picture of the human mind.

Underlying Networks of Associations

If so much important activity goes on unconsciously, then how does it happen? According to many researchers, it is based on cognitive associations between umpteen concepts within a very complex network housed below the conscious level of awareness.[11]

The idea of cognitive associations is not new. Around 400-300 B.C., Aristotle proposed a variety of ways in which they occur.[12] The most obvious is when similar concepts like *lion and tiger* become associated. But associations can also occur when dissimilar concepts either occur back-to-back in time, like *lightning and thunder*, or side-to-side in physical space, like *pencil and paper*. Either way, the more often such concepts occur together in time or space, the stronger the concepts become linked within an underlying network of associations.

The most popular theory about cognitive associations is the one proposed by Allan Collins and Elizabeth Loftus.[13] They posit that within any person's memory, there is a huge network of associations containing many concepts with a variety of connections between concepts. Figure 2.2 depicts a subset of such a network. The ovals represent the concepts, while the lines between ovals represent the associations. If a line is fairly short, it means the two concepts are strongly associated. If a line is longer it means the two concepts are associated, but the connection is not as strong.

When one concept is activated, in any way, associated concepts will also be activated, at least to some degree. This occurs because the activation spreads within the network. It has a rippling effect along the pathways, similar to a stone that is thrown into a lake. Its effect spreads from the initial plunk. Keep in mind that all this occurs automatically and unconsciously. Thus, these networks explain how subtle, incidental exposure to the word *rabbit* will increase the chances that you will think *hare* when asked to spell "hair or hare."

Many studies have supported these kinds of network theories. Most of them are variations of the old-fashioned free association task. Free association occurs when someone presents a word, and you are supposed to say the first thing that comes to mind. As suggested in Figure 2.2, if someone says *college*, there's a good chance you might say *students* or *campus*, maybe *learning* or *research*. It's unlikely that you would say *gymnasium*. However, it is possible you will eventually think *gymnasium*, because *college* and *gymnasium* are indirectly linked via *campus* and *buildings*.

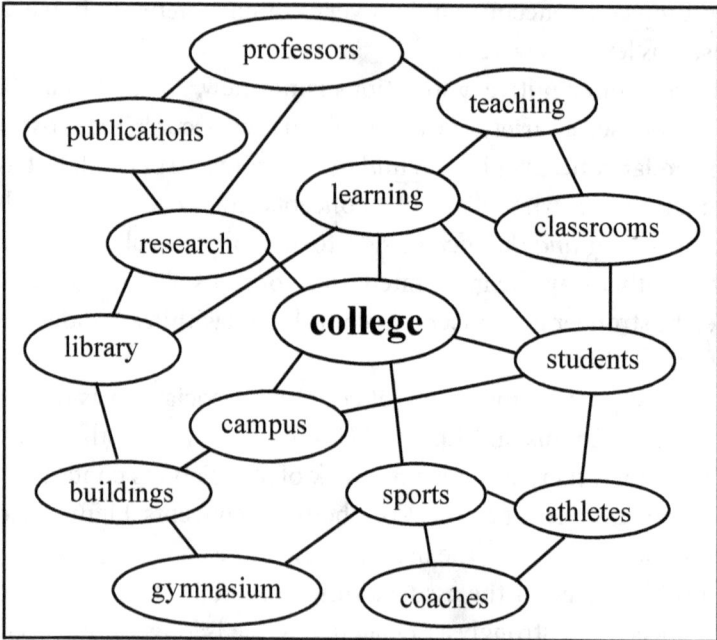

Figure 2.2: Associative Network

The studies that have been most influential are so-called *priming* experiments. In some of these experiments, participants are asked to make a *yes or no* decision as quickly as possible in response to some kind of concept. The concepts are usually words or phrases that are presented via a computer, and they are referred to as the target concepts. The *yes or no* decision is made simply by pressing a button on the computer's keyboard. For example, you might be asked whether or not a group of letters forms a real word in the English language.

Give it a try. Do the letters *geskon* form a word in the English language?

How about *doctor?* How about *field?* How about *pleb?* How about *cat?* Very quickly, you should be able to respond *no* (to *geskon*), *yes* (to *doctor*), *yes* (to *field*), *no* (to *pleb*), and *yes* (to *cat*). Usually participants make such decisions and responses in less than one second, perhaps averaging close to half a second.[14]

The priming occurs when just before the participant needs to make the decision about the target concept, a prime concept is presented for a short period of time, maybe within 1-2 seconds before the target concept is presented. In some research, the prime concept is presented so quickly that it occurs below the threshold for conscious awareness. In these cases, you can consciously perceive a flash of letters, but you cannot be consciously aware that a prime concept occurred as part of the flash. It's called *subliminal priming*. If the prime concept (whether it's presented consciously or unconsciously) is closely associated to the target concept, then participants are usually faster in responding to the target concept.

For the example described above, you would be slightly faster in responding *yes* to *doctor* and *yes* to *cat*, if the prime concepts of *nurse* and *tiger* were presented just moments before. Such results provide convincing evidence that related concepts *(nurse → doctor* and *tiger → cat)* are closely associated within a person's underlying network of cognitive associations. Subtle activation of one concept automatically spreads to the other concept.

One of my favorite quotes about the human mind comes from cognitive scientist Donald Norman: "Mental life is not neat and orderly. It does not proceed smoothly and gracefully in neat, logical form. Instead, it hops, skips, and jumps its way from idea to idea, tying together things that have no business being put together."[15]

But is this true? Consciously, it seems to be true. That's because consciously, it occasionally seems illogical how two thoughts got linked together, as if it were by accident. But unconsciously, and within an underlying network of associations, shouldn't there always be an orderly sequence of mental events?

Today, associative network theories are quite complex. Some researchers propose that emotions or emotional responses can be represented within such networks. And other researchers propose that behavioral responses are also included.[16] Thus, (1) how we perceive situations and other people – in positive or negative ways, (2) how we start to feel emotionally, (3) how we manifest subtle, yet noticeable expressions – facial expressions and body posture, and (4) how we outwardly respond in other ways to various situations and people, can all be initiated and occur at the unconscious level of awareness.

An Analogy

The best way to understand the relationship between our two levels of conscious awareness and how things get done within the human mind, is to use an analogy – in this case, the analogy of how the executive branch of a government might operate and get things done.[17] So consider, if our conscious level would be like a president, or chief executive, in a governing body, then what kind of president would it be? Also, what would be the role of all the other people who work with the president in making decisions and exercising executive control? They too would work within the executive branch, but presumably under the president's leadership.

There are three main possibilities. First, perhaps the president, our consciousness, would be a chief executive, who is *completely in charge*. In this case, the president would set priorities and initiate all decisions, including day-to-day decisions. Then she or he would delegate responsibilities to lower-level personnel for the actual execution of the decisions. This analogy would suggest consciousness is indeed an important decision-maker, setting priorities and being very much involved in day-to-day activities. It also suggests that our unconscious level of awareness would be subservient, important in carrying out activities, but not so important in initiating the decisions to do so.

Second, maybe the president, our consciousness, would be a chief executive who simply *sets priorities and some long-term goals*. Presumably such priorities and goals would be based on a set of values. (How the values would be determined is a good question.) Then it would be all the lower-level personnel under the president who actually initiate the important day-to-day decisions and carryout corresponding activities. This kind of president would still have daily responsibilities. She or he would (1) occasionally remind people about the priorities and (2) provide explanations for why things occur the way they do. Most likely this kind of president would also take credit for everything that happens, even though it's debatable whether she or he actually initiated anything specific.

This analogy suggests that what goes on consciously is less important for day-to-day decisions, beyond setting general priorities and long-term goals. Our unconscious level of awareness would be much more important. However, consciousness would still be important for describing events and explaining why things happen the way they do. Most likely, these descriptions and explanations would give the impression, and perhaps the illusion, that consciousness is indeed in charge. So over time, consciousness will probably take credit for virtually all behavior. In a sense this might not be wrong, since consciousness set priorities that presumably filtered down to lower-level decisions.

Third, perhaps consciousness within an executive branch of a government is not like the president or chief executive at all. Instead, perhaps it is like the press secretary for the president – the person who simply describes things that are going on and tries to explain why. In this view, the unconscious level would be more important than the conscious level. Now unconscious processing would run the show, and consciousness would only describe and explain things, and in doing so, have the impression that it is in charge more than it is.

Which analogy is correct – (1) consciousness in charge, along with describing and explaining things, (2) consciousness only setting priorities but still describing and explaining things, or (3) consciousness only describing and explaining things? This is a good question. Before reading this book, you would probably vote for the first possibility. It feels correct. But more and more researchers are proposing that something like the third possibility might be more accurate – that consciousness is mostly like a press secretary within an executive branch of government. As Jonathan Haidt suggests, "Once human beings developed language [in the evolutionary process] and began to use it to gossip about each other, it became extremely valuable for [all of us to have] a full-time public relations firm."[18]

The purpose of this book is not to choose among these three possibilities. I will, however, continue to make the case that what goes on unconsciously is much more important than we realize. Then hopefully, you will at least be intrigued with the possibility that the third alternative is correct. If not, then perhaps the second alternative represents a nice compromise.

Chapter 3

Do We Really Know What We Believe?
"The Implicit Association Test"

"I consider extremely fruitful this idea that social life should be explained
not by the notions of those who participate in it,
but by more profound causes which are unperceived by consciousness."
– Émile Durkheim

During the 1990s, several researchers started taking a new look at what it means to believe something. Whenever a person believes something there are aspects of the belief that show up consciously. That's the obvious part. But there must also be aspects that occur unconsciously, and it is likely those aspects are important.

The kinds of beliefs that researchers were interested in were beliefs that are personal and sensitive in nature. For such beliefs, researchers argued that you cannot always trust what someone says about their beliefs. This is not because they necessarily lie or stretch-the-truth, although this probably occurs in some cases. Instead, it is likely that people cannot completely know their beliefs given the complexity of the human mind.[1] As the Russian writer Fyodor Dostoyevsky suggested over 100 years ago,

> Every man has reminiscences which he would not tell to everyone but only his friends. He has other matters in his mind which he would not reveal even to his friends, but only to himself, and that in secret. But there are other things which a man is afraid to tell even to himself, and every decent man has a number of such things stored away in his mind.[2]

So how do researchers investigate the "other things" that are stored away in our minds, lurking beneath the level of conscious awareness? The basic strategy is to have research participants perform a task in which they need to provide their responses very quickly, perhaps within one second. At this speed, it is hard to imagine that participants could be relying on conscious processing to give their responses. Instead, they are probably relying on unconscious processing which is much faster and automatic in nature.

The most popular of these speed tasks is the "Implicit Association Test," initially devised by Anthony Greenwald and Mahzarin Banaji, and hereafter referred to as the IAT.[3] The test almost always involves sitting at a computer and making very fast decisions about concepts that belong to certain categories. It can feel confusing at times, but that's the point. If the task were easy, participants could use conscious processing to override important aspects of beliefs that would otherwise show up unconsciously.

To understand the IAT, consider a variation. Imagine you are given 20 cards or slips of paper, and each one contains either a picture or a word from one of four categories. Let's say the 20 cards contain (1) five pictures of *flowers*, (2) five pictures of *insects*, (3) five words that are considered *pleasant* in nature – for example, *nice, fun, happy,* and (4) five words that are considered *unpleasant* in nature – for example, *yucky, nasty, mad.* Now the cards are shuffled, and your task is to correctly sort them onto two piles as fast as possible.

But the overall task requires that you sort the cards onto two piles, twice, called two phases. During one phase, you must place the flower pictures and the pleasant words together on one pile while placing the insect pictures and the unpleasant words together on the other pile. During a separate phase, you must place the flower pictures and the unpleasant words together on one pile while placing the insect pictures and the pleasant words together on the other pile. (These two phases are interchanged when different people perform the task.) If you are like most people you will find this task much easier during the phase when you need to combine the flower pictures with the pleasant words on a pile, and insect pictures with unpleasant words on another pile. You will find it harder during the phase when you need to combine the flower pictures with the unpleasant words and insect pictures with pleasant words.

The reason this occurs is because flowers are considered more pleasant and insects are considered more unpleasant in our unconscious minds. Specifically, researchers argue that the concepts of flowers are more closely related, or more strongly related, to pleasant concepts within the networks of associations in our unconscious minds, compared to unpleasant concepts. Similarly, the concepts of insects are more closely related, or more strongly related, to unpleasant concepts, compared to pleasant concepts.

Almost all IAT's are administered using a computer. Computers allow researchers to measure how fast participants perform at each step within the task. During a computer-based IAT, participants use two fingers with two response keys to group various concepts presented on the computer's monitor. Sometimes they only need to evaluate two categories at a time. That's the easy part. At other times, they need to evaluate four categories while still using only two fingers and corresponding response keys. This is essentially the same as placing concepts from four categories onto two piles. This is also when it gets challenging, because participants must combine concepts from two of the categories with one finger (perhaps flowers and pleasant words) and concepts from the remaining two categories (perhaps insects and unpleasant concepts) with the other finger. When the pairs of categories that need to be grouped together are closely related, then the task is much easier than when the pairs of categories are very different.

Stereotypic Beliefs

The most common way in which the IAT has been used is to evaluate underlying biases about racial stereotypes, in particular biases for African Americans compared to Caucasian Americans. Participants usually need to group concepts from the categories of *African Americans, Caucasian Americans, positive concepts, and negative concepts.* The consistent finding is that Caucasian participants who consciously report that they do not harbor any racial biases, nonetheless show an unconscious preference for Caucasians compared to African Americans when evaluated via the IAT.

Figure 3.1 provides an example how these categories, *African Americans, Caucasian Americans, positive concepts, and negative concepts,* might be presented in an actual experiment. In real research only one concept is presented at a time. The stereotypic names and concepts in this example are a subset of those used in the original IAT research conducted by Anthony Greenwald and colleagues.[4]

Instructions for Figure 3.1: For Panel 1, use one hand to point to stereotypically Caucasian names and positive concepts, while using the other hand (simultaneously) to point to stereotypically African American names and negative concepts. For Panel 2, use one hand to point to stereotypically African American names and positive concepts, while using the other hand (simultaneously) to point to stereotypically Caucasian names and negative concepts.

Panel 1: Caucasian+Positive AfricanAmerican+Negative	Panel 2: AfricanAmerican+Positive Caucasian+Negative
Amber	poison
sickness	Stephen
vacation	Temeka
Jerome	laughter
sunrise	Heather
Latoya	cheer
divorce	Terrance
Bradley	agony

Figure 3.1: An IAT Example

Virtually all Caucasians find it easier to respond quickly and accurately during the phase in which *Caucasian American and positive concepts* are combined and *African American and negative concepts* are combined; see Panel 1. They find it harder to perform as well during the phase in which *Caucasian American and negative concepts* are combined and *African American and positive concepts* are combined; see Panel 2. Such results do not occur at random or by magic. Instead, they occur because virtually all Caucasian Americans, whether they realize it or not, have fostered an unconscious preference for Caucasians compared to African Americans.[5]

Several researchers refer to such unconscious biases as "ordinary prejudice." Thus, the results described above should not be surprising. We should expect people to have unconscious biases toward those who are perceived as different, however the difference shows up. As Mahzarin Banaji says, "It is a byproduct of the ordinary ways in which we think and feel and learn."[6]

If you want to try a real IAT, you can do so at *https://implicit.harvard. edu/implicit.* There are several versions at this site including the Race IAT with African Americans being compared with Caucasian Americans. But you can also compare *young people* to *old people* – the Age IAT, *heavy people* to *thin people* – the Weight IAT, *females* to *males* – the Gender IAT, and even *former presidents of the United States* to *each other* – the Presidents IAT.

These IAT tasks have become quite popular. Several years ago, the Race IAT was featured during one of the episodes of the television show *King of the Hill.*[7] During this episode, the family dog bites an African American person who was visiting the house. As a result, several people accuse the owner of the dog to be a "racist," because they believe the dog was somehow picking up subtle and negative cues from the owner. Eventually a friend suggests that the owner takes the Race IAT to presumably get at the deep-down truth. Is the owner of the dog innocent or guilty with respect to underlying racist beliefs?

Whatever the version, the IAT is always a speed task, and it can be treated like a game. Of course, as you are doing it, you will be evaluated. For which types of people might you have stronger underlying associations with positive concepts, and for which types of people might you have stronger underlying associations with negative concepts?

Conceptions of Self

Another common way in which the IAT has been used is to evaluate a person's unconscious self-esteem or unconscious sense-of-self, when compared to others. Figures 3.2 and 3.3 present a short paper-and-pencil version for you to try. Such versions are rarely used in actual research, but they can give you an idea of what it would be like to be a participant in an actual experiment. It only takes about 2-3 minutes, so get a pencil and give it a try. It is designed to provide an evaluation of *self*, compared to *others*, at the unconscious level of awareness.[8]

> Instructions for Figure 3.2: Panel 1 presents eight practice trials. The first two are completed for you. Place a dash (or checkmark) to the left of each word that is either a "self" term (me, my, mine) or a positive modifier (i.e., adjective

or adverb). Place a dash (or checkmark) to the right of each word that is either an "other" term (they, them, their) or a negative modifier (i.e., adjective or adverb). Panel 2 presents eight additional practice trials, but they are different. Again, the first two are completed for you. For Panel 2, place a dash (or checkmark) to the left of each word that is either a "self" term (me, my, mine) or a negative modifier (i.e., adjective or adverb). Place a dash (or checkmark) to the right of each word that is either an "other" term (they, them, their) or a positive modifier (i.e., adjective or adverb).

Panel 1: Practice		Panel 2: Practice	
"Self" Term	"Other" Term	"Self" Term	"Other" Term
or + Modifier	or - Modifier	or - Modifier	or + Modifier
	rotten---		--- useless
---my			them---
	they		me
	healthy		evil
	mine		proper
	their		they
	filthy		mine
	worthy		good

Figure 3.2: IAT Practice

Instructions for Figure 3.3: Now the test phase! On the two panels in Figure 3.3, try to categorize (and appropriately check) the words as quickly as possible, and time yourself. Estimate how long it takes to correctly categorize the 22 words in Panel 3, by putting dashes/checkmarks to the left or to the right in the same way as in Panel 1. Then estimate how long it takes to correctly categorize the 22 words in Panel 4, by putting dashes/checkmarks to the left or to the right in the same way as in Panel 2.

Panel 3: Test Phase 1		Panel 4: Test Phase 2	
"Self" Term or + Modifier	"Other" Term or - Modifier	"Self" Term or - Modifier	"Other" Term or + Modifier
	mine		they
	useless		filthy
	their		me
	rotten		them
	they		good
	me		mine
	them		my
	valid		useless
	my		healthy
	proper		their
	mine		mine
	good		good
	they		they
	evil		valid
	worthy		their
	bad		evil
	them		proper
	healthy		useless
	me		me
	valid		healthy
	filthy		them
	their		valid

Figure 3.3: IAT Evaluation of Self

You just completed a paper-and-pencil version of the IAT. In real research, participants receive more practice (Panels 1 & 2) than you received. Thus, the test phases (Panels 3 & 4) do not feel quite as confusing. Remember, the test phases are supposed to feel confusing, so a person cannot over-rely on conscious processing to give their responses.

If you are like most people, you found it easier to categorize words correctly in the *self terms with positive modifiers phase* (the first test phase) than the *self terms with negative modifiers phase* (the second test phase). The degree to which the first phase (self terms with positive modifiers) was easier than the second phase (self terms with negative modifiers) provides an indication of your unconscious pro-self bias, compared to others. However, it should be noted that participants usually find the first phase slightly easier than the second phase, whenever they perform an IAT. Thus, if you really want an accurate indication of your unconscious sense-of-self, you should try the test several times on different days and mix-up the order of the two test phases each time you take the test.

To understand how such pro-self preferences occur, consider a variation of the Collins and Loftus' associative network theory described in chapter 2. See Figure 3.4. It depicts part of a theory put forth by Greenwald, Banaji, and other colleagues.[9]

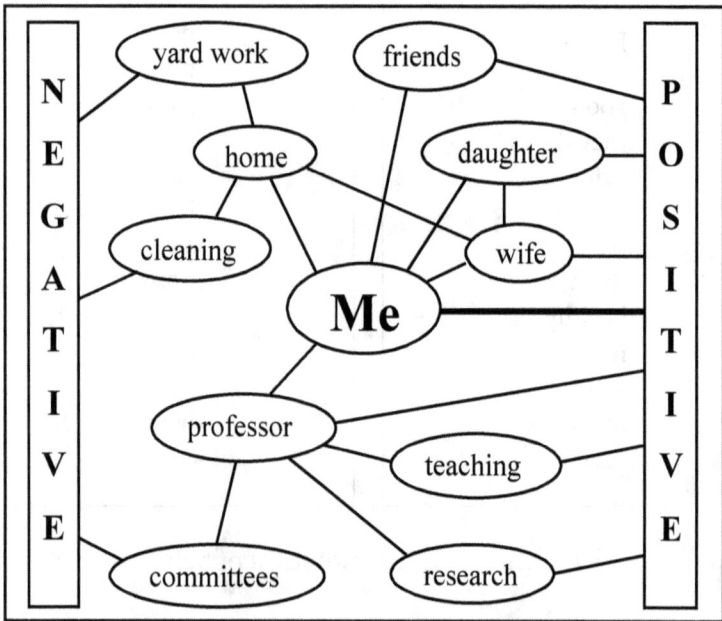

Figure 3.4: Associative Network with Evaluations

What makes this theory different is that it includes negative and positive evaluations at opposite ends of the network, and it depicts a person's concept of self ("Me") in the center. For almost everyone, this concept of self is strongly associated with the positive side. (Note the solid line connected to the positive side.) Then similar to the Collins and Loftus' theory, there are various other concepts within the network along with associations between the concepts. The associations have varying strengths to each other and to either the negative or positive direction. The strengths are fostered based on our real-world experiences, and this includes how we think about concepts in either negative or positive ways.

For my underlying network of associations (the one depicted in Figure 3.4), I am sure I would have very strong connections to my wife and daughter – both being very positive in nature. However, I confess I do not particularly like committees and committee work. But as you consider my underlying network of associations, consider also how your network might look. Think too, about the people with whom you have very strong disagreements. Where might they be located? For me, some of them would be connected to the negative side, perhaps as directly as "yard work, cleaning, and committees."

Chapter 4

Unconscious Content: It Matters

"Most of a person's everyday life is determined
not by their conscious intentions and deliberate choices,
but by mental processes that are put into motion
by features of the environment and that operate
outside of conscious awareness and guidance."
– John Bargh and Tanya Chartrand,
"The Unbearable Automaticity of Being"

Most likely all researchers believe that at some point in time, the content within our underlying networks of associations will be activated, at least to some degree. The more important question, however, is whether or not the content will eventually make a difference in what we do.

In an influential article entitled "The Cognitive Monster," John Bargh proposes that quite a bit of the content within the unconscious part of our minds involves negativity, usually based on stereotypes. And he argues that the effects are inevitable. The negative content will either affect how we perceive people or how we respond to people, or perhaps how we react in certain situations. To emphasize this point, Bargh likens the negativity to "cognitive monsters that cannot be caged."[1]

There have been many experiments demonstrating how negative content – cognitive monsters – can have subsequent effects on behavior. The most intriguing ones have involved subliminal perception. In such research, participants are exposed to information in a way that they cannot be consciously aware of all that is being presented. The question is whether or not any of the information might still have an effect on how they feel or respond in a subsequent situation.

Using subliminal perception is a great research strategy, because whatever the effect is, it must have involved cognitive processes that occurred unconsciously. Patricia Devine's research, conducted at Ohio State University, is the classic demonstration.[2] In her research, Caucasian college students were led to believe that they were participating in three separate studies. In reality, they were participating in a single experiment with three different phases.

During the first phase, all participants responded to a survey that evaluated their attitudes toward African Americans. Presumably this involves quite a bit of conscious processing since participants can be aware of how they are responding. Virtually all the participants reported that they have very little, if any, biases against African Americans. Essentially, they reported that they see African Americans and Caucasian Americans as the same.

During the second phase, participants performed what seemed to be a simple reaction-time task. Sitting at a computer, all they needed to do was identify as quickly as possible, whether a flash of random letters appeared to the left on the computer's monitor or to the right on the monitor. The flashes of letters only lasted two-tenths of a second. The computers were programmed so the letters would either appear toward the top-left, lower-left, top-right, or bottom-right of the monitor, in random order. It's a basic perceive-and-respond task. All the participants need to do is press a computer key to the left if the flash is toward the left, or a computer key to the right if the flash is to the right. Easy enough.

What participants did not realize was that for half of them, words appeared as part of the flash of random letters. The words included terms such as *welfare, blues, civil rights, ghetto,* et cetera – terms that are stereotypically associated with African Americans. These words appeared for the first half of the two-tenths of a second that the flash appeared to either the left or the right. This constitutes subliminal priming, because when participants are asked if they saw any words as part of the perceive-and-respond task, they almost always say "No." And if by chance they say "Yes," they have difficulty identifying what the words were.

During the third phase, and again ostensibly unrelated to the previous phases, the participants were asked to evaluate a hypothetical person in a story. The person's name was Donald. In the story, Donald did some things that may or may not be considered inappropriate and negative in nature. In part of the story, he confronts a cashier at a store's checkout counter while shopping, and in another part, he refuses to pay the rent for his apartment until a certain improvement is made. In both cases, it is impossible to know for sure, whether or not Donald's behavior might actually be warranted and appropriate. For example, perhaps he was over-charged during the shopping episode, and perhaps his apartment indeed needs improvement. On the other hand, perhaps Donald is a bit quick-tempered and his behavior is inappropriate.

Results indicated that participants who were subliminally exposed to words associated with African Americans, just moments before hearing the story about Donald, tended to evaluate Donald more negatively and see his behavior as inappropriate. Participants who were not subliminally exposed to words associated with African Americans, did not evaluate Donald as negatively, and they were more likely to consider the possibility that his behavior might be warranted and appropriate. It's sobering. Negative content that we do not even realize we have, can be activated and affect what we do, unconsciously.

A similar experiment was conducted by Bargh and colleagues at New York University.[3] They too had Caucasian college students perform a perceive-and-respond task that simply required that they identify certain patterns within a computer display. However, while performing the task, half of the participants were briefly exposed to pictures of African American males. The exposure only lasted about 1/75th of a second, and it occurred just before they needed to identify and respond to the pattern. At that speed, participants cannot consciously perceive the faces.

After each participant completed the perceive-and-respond task, an assistant of the researchers approached the participant and informed them that there was an error in how the computer recorded their information. Because of this error, they would need to perform the task all over again. Such an inconvenience causes frustration. To evaluate the degree of frustration, the researchers videotaped each participant's response. Results indicated that participants who were subliminally exposed to faces of African American males during the perceive-and-respond task demonstrated more frustration and more anger to the inconvenience, than the participants who were not subliminally exposed to the faces.

These kinds of studies have important implications. All of us have negative unconscious baggage that we have fostered over the years, and there's a good chance that the negativity is directed toward certain types of people, whether African Americans or not. Simply put, none of us is pure. Consciously we can convince ourselves that the negativity doesn't exist, let alone believe that it could affect us in some way. But unconsciously, it does exist – ala "cognitive monsters." If the negativity is primed, based on subtle cues, it can indeed influence our subsequent judgments and behaviors. Unconscious content: it matters!

Incidental Priming Research

While subliminal perception experiments have been interesting and intriguing, many more experiments have used what is generally considered to be "incidental priming." In these experiments, participants can be aware of the priming that is going on, but they are not aware of how the priming might affect subsequent behavior. Thus, researchers argue that whatever cognitive processing is involved with the overall priming and subsequent behavior, a large amount of it must be unconscious.

Consider four examples, the first three of which were conducted at New York University under the leadership of John Bargh. In a humorous experiment, the researchers induced participants to temporarily think about *elderly people*.[4] Participants were instructed to devise sentences using sets of five words – construct grammatically-correct sentences using four out of five words that were given for each sentence. It's called a "Scrambled Sentence Test." Give it a try. As quickly as possible, construct a 4-word sentence using the words, *he, it, hides, finds, instantly.* Your answer is . . . ?

For half of the participants, the words that needed to be used were concepts related to elderly people – words such as *old, grey, retired, wise, wrinkle,* and *bingo.* The other participants were not exposed to such elderly concepts. After participants were finished with the Scrambled Sentence Test, an assistant of the researchers recorded how fast each participant walked as they left the experimental room. Specifically, the assistant timed how fast each one walked for the first ten yards after they left the room. The participants who were exposed to words related to elderly people tended to walk more slowly than the participants who were not exposed to the elderly words. It is unlikely that any of these participants, the ones exposed to the elderly concepts, were aware of how the underlying priming set them up to behave the way they did.

In a related experiment, the researchers used the same Scrambled Sentence Test to prime the concepts of either *politeness or rudeness*.[5] As in the previous experiment, participants made up sentences that were grammatically correct using four out of five words that were given for each sentence. In doing so, half of the participants needed to consider using words related to politeness, such as *respect, honor, patiently,* and *cordially.* The other half needed to consider using words related to rudeness, such as *disturb, bother, intrude,* and *aggressively.*

At the beginning of the experiment, all participants were told that when they were finished with the sentence-completion task, they should go to another room to get the experimenter. Apparently at that point, the experimenter would tell them what to do for the second part of the experiment. But everything was staged so that when each participant went to get the experimenter, the experimenter was talking with another person and positioned with his or her back toward the participant. Results indicated that participants who were incidentally exposed to the words related to *rudeness* were three times more likely to interrupt the conversation within a 10-minute time period, and they did so in about half the time, compared to participants who were incidentally exposed to words related to *politeness.*

Our positive or negative tendencies can be primed in a variety of ways. In a third experiment at New York University, researchers used a subtle environmental cue to influence how participants might evaluate a stranger they were about to meet.[6] As participants showed up for the experiment, they were greeted by a research assistant who escorted them to the psychology lab via an elevator. While in the elevator, the assistant politely asked participants to briefly hold a cup of coffee so the assistant could take notes as they talked. For half of the participants, the cup of coffee was very warm. For the other half, the cup of coffee was very cold.

When they reached the psychology lab, participants were asked to evaluate the personality of a fictional character who was only described as intelligent, skilled, and hard-working. The participants who had briefly held the warm cup of coffee tended to rate the fictional person as more friendly and generous than the participants who briefly held the cold cup of coffee. So very subtle cues in the environment can play a role in how we unconsciously process information about people and form subsequent judgments – in this case, the degree to which we consider a person friendly or not. Parenthetically, the temperature of the cup of coffee did not influence how participants rated the fictional person on characteristics that were less related to friendliness, such as physical attractiveness and talkativeness.

For the fourth example of incidental priming, consider a humorous study conducted by Ap Dijksterhuis and Ad van Knippenberg at the University of Nijmegen in the Netherlands. Their research has a great subtitle: "How to Win a Game of Trivial Pursuit."[7] In one of their experiments, participants were asked to spend five minutes identifying characteristics of a typical college professor and to focus on those characteristics. In another experiment, participants were asked to spend five minutes identifying characteristics of hooligans at European football (American soccer) competitions and to focus on those characteristics. In both cases, participants were told to write about the characteristics they were considering.

All participants were then asked to take a quiz involving general knowledge questions – questions that you might get in a game like *Trivial Pursuit*. The participants who spent time focusing on the characteristics of college professors performed better in answering the general knowledge questions compared to those who spent time focusing on the characteristics of troublemakers at sporting events.

Again, exposure to information and processing the information, consciously and unconsciously, can affect us in ways we do not realize. As part of their research, Dijksterhuis and van Knippenberg provide a story to further explain how their results occurred:

> Some time ago, a few members of the Department of Social Psychology of the University of Nijmegen visited a soccer match. After they parked their car, they walked the remaining mile to the stadium. The psychologists, behaving calmly and orderly as ever, were surrounded by hundreds of soccer fans and hooligans, many of whom were yelling and shouting. After some time, one of the members of the department engaged in somewhat unusual behavior. He saw an empty beer can, and, in what seemed to be an impulsive act, he kicked it as far away as possible. During the next few minutes, he and a slightly embarrassed colleague pondered on possible explanations. One explanation is that, upon seeing soccer hooligans (or simply thinking about soccer hooli-

gans), one may – without being aware of it – start to act like them. That is, the activation of the representation of soccer hooligans leads to a tendency to behave similarly.[8]

A 1-2-3 Sequence

Occasionally you hear stories about how a person misspeaks, puts their foot in their mouth, or performs some other spontaneous and embarrassing behavior. When this happens to a public figure, perhaps a politician, sports hero, or media celebrity, it often becomes newsworthy. Also, the behaviors can be pretty severe in nature. Perhaps you can remember times when a public figure has either punched someone, inappropriately hand-gestured someone, swore at someone, or insulted someone (or a group of people) in some other way. Perhaps you also remember that after such embarrassing moments, the culprit often apologizes and tries to claim "That's not me, and that is not what I stand for!"

But such negativity indeed represents something about the person. These spontaneous behaviors do not occur by magic. They occur because the person has fostered some amount of negative content within their underlying network of associations along with possible negative responses. The negativity might have been fostered intentionally or inadvertently. Either way, the probability for perceiving negativity and then either swearing, hand-gesturing, making insulting remarks, or doing some other inappropriate behavior, will necessarily correspond with the degree to which the person has already practiced the perceptions and the behaviors in the past.

In an article entitled "The Unbearable Automaticity of Being," Bargh and Chartrand use a baseball analogy to describe how a sequence of unconscious events can take place to produce a behavior. They emphasize how (1) the presentation of certain environmental cues can (2) activate a perception of the cues, which in turn (3) activates a behavioral tendency. And they say it can become as routine as a 1-2-3 double play in baseball – the shortstop to the secondbaseman to the firstbaseman.

In the early 1900s, Joe Tinker, Johnny Evers, and Frank Chance were three players on the Chicago Cubs who became famous for their proficiency in turning such double plays. Thus, Bargh and Chartrand state that "[1] environment to [2] perception to [3] behavior operates as efficiently and smoothly in producing social behavior as the legendary Chicago Cubs infielders did in producing double plays."[9] Tinker to Evers to Chance, and you're out! Environment to perception to behavior, and you might be embarrassed!

Recently, I experienced two of my own real-world examples of the 1-2-3, "environment to perception to behavior" sequence. Thankfully, neither is embarrassing. The first occurred during the winter holiday season when my wife was playing a new James Taylor Christmas CD she had purchased. She's a big James Taylor fan, but it must have been at least five years since I remember listening to any of his music. After hearing a few of his Christmas songs, without thinking about it, I started whistling "I've seen fire and I've seen rain," which is probably Taylor's most famous song. How did I go from hearing Christmas music to whistling "I've seen fire and I've seen rain?" I submit that it occurred via a sequence of unconscious activations associated with James Taylor.

The second example occurred during a day when my wife and I were helping some friends move from one home to another. We used our car to transport some of their stuff, while our friends traveled separately in the truck they had rented. The moving venture required two trips. During the first trip, we traveled on a road that we knew but rarely use. Then later, as we were unloading the first loads from the truck and our car, I momentarily found myself thinking about an acquaintance from about 20 years earlier. Why in the world would I now be thinking of this old-time acquaintance who is completely unrelated to what I was doing at the moment? The person I was thinking about was a former player from my old softball-playing days, and I'm pretty sure I had never thought about him for at least the last ten years.

Then as my wife and I were helping with the second truckload and carload, we again traveled on that rarely used road. This time I consciously noticed a *Home For Sale* sign along the road. The sign had this person's picture and name on it. Guess what? He's a real-estate agent. Now all this makes sense. I am sure that I unconsciously perceived that *Home For Sale* sign the first time we traveled on the road I mentioned. The sign served as an incidental environmental cue, and it was perceived, but not consciously. The reason I was eventually thinking of this person while unloading the first car and truck loads, was because that unconscious perception activated the tendency to think about the person. A 1-2-3 sequence: environmental cue to perception to behavioral tendency.

A Challenge

If the content within our underlying networks of associations can be activated and make a difference in what we do, then are there things we can do to minimize the chances that any of this occurs negatively? Yes, and consider two possibilities.

First, we must be careful about fostering inappropriate negativity in the first place, or at least careful about fostering any additional negativity to what we already have. As described, such negativity can be based on (1) exposure to negative stereotypes, whether about African Americans or some other group of people, (2) subtle thoughts about rudeness, or (3) spending time thinking about negative behavior, such as that of soccer hooligans. Avoiding all such negativity is probably impossible, but it might be worth the effort.

There are studies to indicate that negative content is learned faster than positive content, and that negativity persists longer than favorable information. Once it is learned, unconscious negativity can be very hard to reverse, or as some researchers say, "[It's] easier done than undone."[10] With conscious efforts, however, it's likely we can at least keep some of this in check.

Second, perhaps we can balance or somehow over-ride negative content with additional positive content. Gordon Logan has suggested that all of the information we have been exposed to in our lives can get stored in our memories or within our underlying networks of associations as so-called "instances."[11] If this is the case, then having more positive instances associated with any given person, compared to negative instances, should increase the chances that we perceive the person and respond to the person in more favorable ways.

But then how many positive instances might be needed within our underlying networks to outweigh the possible effects of negative content? If negative content is learned faster and persists longer as noted above, it certainly has advantages over positive content. Thus, expecting only two or three positive instances to somehow outweigh every negative instance might not be enough.

In *Why Marriages Succeed or Fail,* John Gottman has suggested that whenever one partner in a close relationship makes a negative statement or critical remark to the other partner, they should then balance that negative instance with at least five positive statements or five positive instances, to maintain a healthy relationship.[12] If this is the case, then it makes sense to suggest that whenever we entertain one negative thought about a given person – one negative instance – we should probably balance it with at least five positive thoughts about the person – five positive instances – to maintain a fair balance within our underlying networks of associations. Whether it should be five or not, can be debated. The point is that only having a few positive instances to balance every negative instance is probably not good enough to make a noticeable difference in negative tendencies.

Chapter 5

Love the Sinner? Hate the Sin?

"I remember Christian teachers telling me long ago that I must
hate a bad man's actions, but not hate the bad man
—or, as they would say, hate the sin but not the sinner . . .
How could you hate what a man did and not hate the man?"
– C.S. Lewis, *Mere Christianity*

One of the best ways we can convince ourselves that we are good is to think we can appreciate and respect all people, including those with whom we have major disagreements. Some of us go further. We think we can actually love all such people. If it can be done, then that's impressive. But some of us go further still. We think that we can even love someone who is involved in something we hate, or as some people say, "I can love the sinner and hate the sin."

Is it really possible to have very positive feelings for someone who is associated with an activity that we strongly dislike? Certainly statements to this effect are easy to make. And it is probably easy to convince ourselves, consciously, that we are doing such things. But what about our unconscious level of awareness?

Most likely there are several ways to define what it means to "love the sinner and hate the sin." At minimum, I propose that it means we are maintaining very positive sentiments for someone who is engaged in, or associated with, a behavior for which we have very negative sentiments.[1] Given the complexity of the human mind and what goes on within our unconscious networks of associations, this might be next to impossible. Consider an example put forth by Richard Beck:

I have a friend who finds cigarette smoking to be, in her words, "a disgusting habit." Consequently, she confesses, that whenever she sees a smoker she struggles with making negative characterizations of that person, such as seeing a total stranger as foolish, unintelligent, or lazy. She recognizes these thoughts [initiated at the unconscious level of awareness] as incompatible with her Christian commitment to love others and she resists these thoughts [at the conscious level of awareness]. It is just very, very hard to loathe smoking and not make automatic, largely involuntary, negative characterizations of those who smoke.[2]

Let's broaden that last statement: "It is just very, very hard to loathe [an action – whether it be smoking, a presumed sin, or something else we dislike] and not make automatic, largely involuntary, negative characterizations of those who [do it]."[3]

Networks of Associations

In chapter 2, I described how a lot of information is stored unconsciously within our cognitive networks of associations. In chapter 4, I described research indicating that whatever is stored within such networks plays a role in how we perceive people and how we respond to people. It matters.

Consider an old-fashioned word association task. I will present a word and you say the first thing that comes to your mind. If I present the word *thief*, there's a good chance you will say *steal*. Note that *thief* represents the presumed sinner and *steal* represents the corresponding sin. Thus, it's likely that *thief* and *steal* are closely associated within your underlying network of associations. This alone suggests it will always be easy to mix-up the concepts for sinners and sins, thus making it very hard to consistently love the one and hate the other.

Figure 5.1 depicts how the concepts for a sinner and corresponding sin might show up in an underlying network of associations. As noted in chapter 2, several researchers believe that emotional tendencies can also be included within such networks. Thus, I added the concepts of *love* and *hate* to the network. Presumably if a person loves the sinner and hates the sin, then love must be closely connected to the person and hate must be closely connected to the action, as depicted.

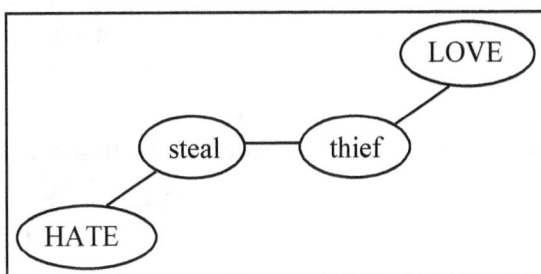

Figure 5.1: Love the Sinner?

There are also researchers who propose that very strong sentiments like love and hate should be represented at opposite ends of the network.[4] Figure 3.4 depicts such a network. If this is the case, then hate might be represented to the extreme left of a large network and love might be represented at the extreme right of the network. Thus, concepts that we dislike would be toward the left with corresponding connections and concepts we like would be toward the right with corresponding connections. But then it would be impossible for the sinner and the corresponding sin to be closely connected to their respective sides – sin to the hate side and sinner to the love side – and still have the two concepts closely connected.

The point is that no matter how convinced we can become that we indeed love someone who is associated with something we strongly dislike, it is more complex than we realize. The unconscious level of awareness must be considered. Most likely we are always capable of an "Oops, I did not mean it that way" *slip-of-the-tongue*, or some other spontaneous behavior to indicate that we do not love the one and hate the other as much as we think.

Almost always, whenever I propose this dilemma of loving someone associated with something we dislike, there is at least one person who says they know it is possible because they have done it. Then they go on to describe how they have a very close friend who is the so-called sinner, the one associated with a very bad behavior. They say they have always loved this friend through-and-through, despite knowing that the friend was involved in something that they hate.

I agree. But this is different. It should always be very doable, and probably easy to love a sinner who is also a friend or close relative. The reason is because our networks of associations contain many concepts and many connections. We probably have many positive connections linked to our friends and family based on the many good experiences we have with them. So whenever we consider the sentiments that exist for any person within our networks, friend or not, we must consider all the possible connections in combination. For those who are very close to us, positive connections probably outweigh any connections that exist based on their bad behavior.

An IAT

If it is possible to love the sinner and hate the sin, unconsciously, then research participants should be able to manifest it via an IAT. I have been involved in two IAT studies. For the first, I teamed up with Amy Daniels, a student at the University of West Alabama. For the second, I teamed up with Kennedy Bota and Peter Odera, professors I worked with during a semester at Masinde Muliro University of Science and Technology in Kenya.[5] In both studies, we had participants quickly categorize words that were either "sinful person" terms (e.g., *thief, cheater, liar*) or "sinful behavior" terms (e.g., *deceive, steal, rape*) with words that were either negative or positive in nature (e.g., *messy, stink, vomit,* and *vacation, joy, flowers,* respectively).

The first study suggested that participants can manifest an unconscious preference for sinful person concepts compared to sinful behavior concepts. But that only indicates that they can favor sinful persons over corresponding behaviors which are probably considered very negative. Favoring the concept of *thief* over the negative action of *stealing* does not necessarily mean participants have positive sentiments for *thief*. It only means they have higher sentiments for *thief* than for *steal*.

In the second study, the one with Bota and Odera, we evaluated participants' sentiments for sinful person and sinful behavior concepts during separate phases. This separation eliminated the direct comparison of sinful persons with sinful behaviors and provided a better indication for the degree to which participants can indeed manifest positive sentiments for so-called sinners at the unconscious level of awareness. Figures 5.2 and 5.3 present a shortened paper-and-pencil version of our IAT.

As noted, paper-and-pencil versions of the IAT are rarely used in actual research, but they can give you a feel for what it would be like to be a real participant. This specific version is called a "Single-Category IAT" because the sinful person concepts are evaluated without a direct comparison to the sinful behavior concepts.[6] It takes only about 2-3 minutes. See how easy it might be to manifest unconscious favorability for concepts related to sinful persons. If you can do it, then it probably represents a step toward loving all sinners, at least to some degree.

> Instructions for Figure 5.2: Panel 1 presents eight practice trials. The first two are completed for you. Place a dash (or checkmark) to the left of each word that is either a "sinner" term (e.g., thief, cheater, liar) or a negative modifier (i.e., adjective or adverb). Place a dash (or checkmark) to the right of each word that is a positive modifier (i.e., adjective or adverb). Panel 2 presents eight additional practice trials, but they are different. Again, the first two are completed for you. For Panel 2, place a dash (or checkmark) to the left of each word that is a negative modifier (i.e., adjective or adverb). Place a dash (or checkmark) to the right of each word that is either a "sinner" term (e.g., thief, cheater, liar) or a positive modifier (i.e., adjective or adverb).

Panel 1: Practice		Panel 2: Practice	
"Sinner" Term			"Sinner" Term
or - Modifier	+ Modifier	- Modifier	or + Modifier
	good ---		--- useless
---liar			burglar ---
rotten			good
healthy			evil
thief			proper
valid			cheater
filthy			bad
cheater			worthy

Figure 5.2: IAT Practice

Instructions for Figure 5.3: Now the test phase! On the two panels in Figure 5.3, try to categorize (and appropriately check) the words as quickly as possible, and time yourself. Estimate how long it takes to correctly categorize the 22 words in Panel 3, by putting dashes/checkmarks to the left or to the right in the same way as in Panel 1. Then estimate how long it takes to correctly categorize the 22 words in Panel 4, by putting dashes/checkmarks to the left or to the right in the same way as in Panel 2. Remember too, the test phases are supposed to feel confusing. This keeps a person from relying on conscious processing, as opposed to relying on what has been fostered unconsciously.

Panel 3: Test Phase 1 "Sinner" Term or - Modifier / + Modifier	**Panel 4: Test Phase 2** "Sinner" Term - Modifier / or + Modifier
worthy	cheater
liar	filthy
evil	thief
cheater	worthy
thief	rotten
good	burglar
filthy	valid
burglar	useless
valid	healthy
liar	good
bad	liar
proper	bad
burglar	thief
rotten	valid
worthy	cheater
useless	evil
cheater	proper
healthy	useless
good	liar
valid	healthy
thief	burglar
rotten	valid

Figure 5.3: IAT Evaluation of Sinners

If you found it easier to categorize words correctly in the second test phase – sinner terms with positive modifiers, compared to the first test phase – sinner terms with negative modifiers, then you have indeed manifested positive unconscious sentiments for sinful people. However, this is contrary to what we found in our research conducted in the United States and Kenya. Virtually all of our participants found it much easier to categorize sinful person terms with negative modifiers than to categorize sinful person concepts with positive modifiers. This suggests that very few, if any of us can indeed manifest unconscious favorability for sinners, let alone love them unconsciously.[7]

It is true that the sinful person terms used in both of our studies suggested very negative behaviors. So it can be debated whether participants would have manifested the same degree of unconscious negativity if the person-related terms only represented concepts that we find frustrating, but not necessarily sinful. It would also be interesting to know how participants might perform on such a task if they were exposed to concepts related to politics and the people with whom they disagree, politically. I am guessing it would still be difficult to manifest positive unconscious sentiments for anyone who is associated with something we strongly dislike, even if it is not a sin.

Chapter 6

The Illusion of an Open Mind

"Open-mindedness is considered to be a virtue. But, strictly speaking,
it cannot occur. A new experience must be redacted into old categories.
We cannot handle each event freshly in its own right.
If we did so, what use would past experience be?"
– Gordon Allport, *The Nature of Prejudice*

I confess. I'm a fan of politics. For quite some time, I've enjoyed watching political debate shows on TV – my all-time favorite being CNN's *Crossfire* which aired during the 1980s and 90s. It was a show that usually pitted two liberal representatives versus two conservatives in discussing some hot-button political issue. So while I have several strong political opinions, those opinions will not be the focus of this chapter. Instead, let's consider how we almost always envision those who agree with us politically as having favorable qualities and those who disagree with us as somehow lacking.

Our current political environment in the United States is very contentious. In *Bee in the Mouth*, Peter Wood argues that it is feistier than ever.[1] Certainly people have been political in the past, passionate in the past, and even angry in the past. What is new, according to Wood, is that a lot of us seem to be proud of our political passion, including occasional "bee in the mouth" outbursts of anger. It is this feistiness that exacerbates our natural tendencies to extend favorable qualities to those with whom we agree, and the opposite to those with whom we disagree.[2]

I am not proposing that anyone should necessarily reduce their passion for politics. There are many issues that are extremely important. But I do propose that all of us take a bit more care in how we envision others, and ourselves, in such a contentious environment.

Cognitive Misers and Monsters

Many researchers propose that the cognitive resources we have for mental activity are always limited, at least to some degree. If that's the case, then we must be careful how we expend the resources. We would not want to think too much, because at some point the thinking will create a strain within our complex, albeit limited, minds. To capture this frugal tendency, researchers have coined the term "cognitive misers."[3] We are misers to the extent that we almost always try to save our cognitive efforts and form opinions in the easiest way possible.

The most common way in which a cognitive miser shows up is in forming opinions about other people. It is so easy for us to quickly identify differences between people, and then use those differences to categorize people into groups. Unfortunately, we rarely stop at that. We also tend to use the differences to generate additional self-esteem – to feel better about ourselves. Thus, we readily evaluate people who are similar to us, in any way possible, as somehow superior and people who are different from us, in any way possible, as somehow inferior – generally referred to as perceptions of "in-group superiority" and "out-group inferiority."[4]

For a demonstration, consider the following hypothetical scenarios, and think how you might respond to each:

> Imagine that tomorrow you meet someone new, a stranger, and you start having a friendly conversation. As part of the conversation, you start talking about politics. In doing so, you realize that this stranger has several political opinions that are very different from your opinions. Most likely, they also have a preference for either the democratic or republican political party, and it differs from your preference. Continue thinking about this person, and consider several issues where you might disagree with this person:
>
> > *War and Military Issues . . .*
> > *Abortion . . .*
> > *Health and Welfare Issues . . .*
> > *Taxes . . .*

Now, how would you guess this person, the stranger you just met, formed his/her political opinions? Certainly some people probably form their political preferences based on their own thinking. You might say that with "internal thinking" they evaluate the pros and cons for various issues and form their own opinions, based on those evaluations. But certainly some people probably form their political preferences based on what you might call "external influences." Perhaps they are influenced by family members or other people they consider important in their lives. For example, conservative-leaning individuals might suggest that left-leaners are primarily influenced by emphases that are presented on television or in public education. Liberal-leaning individuals might suggest that right-leaners are often influenced by emphases of certain religious organizations or radio talk-shows.

Make a guess. How do you think this new person probably formed his/her political preferences? More internally, based on thinking and evaluation of the issues, or more externally, based on influences from others? Use the following scale to check the location for your response. If you suspect more external influence, check a location somewhere to the left. If you suspect more internal thinking, check a location somewhere to the right.

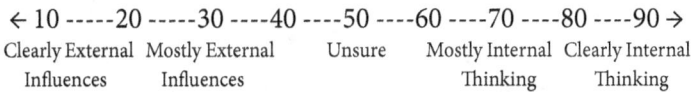

← 10 -----20 -----30 ----40 ----50 ----60 ----70 ----80 ----90 →

| Clearly External | Mostly External | Unsure | Mostly Internal | Clearly Internal |
| Influences | Influences | | Thinking | Thinking |

Now also imagine meeting someone tomorrow, another stranger, who has several political opinions that are very similar to your opinions. Again, most likely this person has a preference for either the democratic or republican political party. How do you think this person formed his/her opinions? More internally, based on careful thought about the pros and cons for various issues, or more externally, based more on influences from others? Think about this person and think about issues such as *War and Military Issues, Abortion, Health and Welfare Issues, Taxes, . . .* Then use the following scale to check the exact location for your response.

← 10 ----20 ----30 ----40 ----50 ----60 -----70 ---- 80 ---- 90 →

Clearly External	Mostly External	Unsure	Mostly Internal	Clearly Internal
Influences	Influences		Thinking	Thinking

If you are like most people, you will have a tendency to score the first person, the one with whom you disagree, more toward the left and score the second person, the one with whom you agree, more toward the right. Thus, you will probably show an automatic tendency to prejudge both people – prejudging the one you disagree with more negatively, assuming they form their political opinions with less thought, and prejudging the one you agree with more favorably, assuming they form their political opinions with more thought.[5]

More than we realize, it is very hard, if not impossible, to be fair and open-minded. As our miserly tendencies suggest, we usually form our opinions with as little cognitive effort as possible, and in self-serving ways to boot.

Some researchers go further. They argue that we are biologically predisposed to be rather narrow-minded and judgmental, at least to some degree, because it has evolutionary value.[6] Whenever we identify any kind of difference between ourselves and another person, no matter how subtle, we automatically suspect other differences as well. And we suspect potential negativity. Doing so helps us identify potential foes more quickly, and over time, this provides a benefit related to survival. In contrast, whenever we identify any kind of similarity between ourselves and another person, again no matter how subtle, we automatically assume additional similarities and positive characteristics. Doing so in this case, helps us identify potential friends more quickly, and over time, this provides another benefit related to survival.

Jeffrey Kluger sums it up this way:

Like all other animals, our species emerged in a world where there was critical value in distinguishing between members of our own tribe – who nurture you and protect you – and members of other tribes, who see you as a competitor . . . Your very survival can turn on making this distinction quickly and reliably; as a result, the primal wiring that makes such discrimination possible is not very easy to disconnect.[7]

So prejudgment is to be expected. Any notions about being completely fair and open-minded are illusory.

Attributional Biases

Several researchers have identified additional tendencies that occur once a person starts to form opinions about who is *similar and better*, and who is *different and not-as-good*. These extra tendencies are termed "attributional biases."[8] They represent the tendencies we have to be more favorable when explaining outcomes for those who are similar to us and less favorable when explaining outcomes for those who differ from us. Here are two classic examples. First, when my side wins, it's because *we are good;* when the other side wins, it's because *they are lucky.* Second, when people like me are successful, it's because *we work hard;* when people unlike me are successful, it's because *they have certain advantages.*

Thomas Pettigrew is more forceful and blunt. Instead of referring to these self-serving tendencies as attributional biases, he says they represent the "ultimate attribution error."[9] Consider possibilities. When a person has beliefs that are similar to my beliefs, then that person is either more thoughtful, better informed, or perhaps more compassionate. On the other hand, when a person has beliefs that are dissimilar to my beliefs, then that person is either less thoughtful, less informed, or perhaps less compassionate. Of course there are people who are less thoughtful, less informed, and less compassionate. So forming such an opinion might not represent an "error," per se, as Pettigrew suggests. However, unless we know for sure, then forming such an opinion represents an assumption – an assumption that is self-serving and unfair.

For quite a while, researchers knew about our tendencies to (1) identify differences between people, (2) to conserve the use of limited cognitive resources, (3) to see ourselves, and our own kind, as superior, and (4) to assume more favorable characteristics for those who are similar and less favorable characteristics for those who are different. But it has only been more recently, that researchers have demonstrated how such tendencies occur unconsciously, and how they represent the foundations of negative stereotypes and negative prejudicial beliefs – again, unconsciously.

In chapter 4, I introduced John Bargh's concept of the "cognitive monster," the negativity that can be maintained within a person's network of associations, under the surface of conscious awareness. Unfortunately, and like a monster, it doesn't always stay hidden beneath that surface. It can indeed affect how we perceive others and how we respond to others.

In describing the "cognitive monster," Bargh presents a light-hearted, yet profound, fable. He emphasizes how our miserly cognitive tendencies combined with negative stereotypic content can yield rather monstrous tendencies. And it can all occur unconsciously and automatically. Here are segments of Bargh's fable:

> Once upon a time, in the land of Social Psychology, there lived the Cognitive Miser . . . [which] was afflicted with the curse of Limited Processing Resources, and therefore . . . it was necessary and wise for the creature to depend on simplifying modes of thought, in order to conserve its constrained mental capacity for when it was most needed. The Cognitive Miser never learned [much about others] as separate individuals, but only reacted to each of them on the basis of their superficial aspects and the roles they played in daily life. It was unfortunate, but a reasonable strategy for the Miser to pursue, given its limits.

> But then [with the advent of negative stereotypes] . . . the Cognitive Miser had been transformed . . . into the Cognitive Monster. No longer did the creature use simplifying categories and stereotypes by choice or strategy; their use had become an addiction – uncontrollable, not a matter of choice at all – and the creature's Will was powerless to do anything else.[10]

It is naïve to think that we will always be able to keep such negative tendencies in check. We simply cannot always allocate enough cognitive resources to avoid slip-ups or any other indications of our underlying biases. As Bargh suggests, a cognitive monster can only be caged so long. He says, "When the populace becomes complacent and lets its guard down, the monster bursts its bonds and rampages again."[11]

Now let's take a stab at a new fable, a variation of Bargh's "Cognitive Monster." This one is about the "Land of Political Passion" in the United States. It illustrates what is going on among those of us who are committed to either the political left or political right. While we appear to be very nice and respectful to each other when we meet in the public square, nonetheless, in private we foster underlying beliefs that correspond with the "Cognitive Monster."

> Once upon a time in the *Land of Political Passion*, there was great political tension and there lived many kinds of Cognitive Misers. These miserly creatures were a natural part of all humans – including people who adhered to the political left and those who adhered to the political right. They were afflicted with the curse of Limited Processing Resources, so they depended on simplified modes of thought, in order to conserve mental capacity for when it might be needed otherwise. Thus, they never learned much about other types of people as separate individuals, but only reacted to them on the basis of superficial characteristics.

> Furthermore, the Misers on the political left and political right started to live at opposite ends in the Land of Political Passion. Oh but they were polite and proper with each other when meeting by happenstance. But privately they believed each other to be rather deficient – wrongheaded and generally lacking in either intelligence or compassion. It seemed a reasonable strategy for the Misers to pursue, given their priorities and their limits.

> But then the Cognitive Misers on the political left and political right became transformed, by the magic of habitual tendencies, into Cognitive Monsters. No longer did the creatures use simplifying categories and stereotypes by choice or

strategy; now their use had become addictions – uncontrollable, not a matter of choice at all – and the Wills of the creatures were powerless to do anything else. The transformed Monsters readily assumed themselves superior – intelligent, compassionate, and the very best people in the Land of Political Passion. Unfortunately, those who lived on the other side of the Land were readily assumed inferior.

Supportive Data

Let's return to the demonstration task at the beginning of this chapter. In a study I conducted as part of a classroom demonstration, college students responded to the same scenarios I proposed for you: Imagine meeting a stranger with whom you either disagree or agree politically. Then think about the person and evaluate how you believe they might have formed their political opinions. Like you, students responded to a scale ranging from 10 (Clearly External Influences) to 50 (Unsure) to 90 (Clearly Internal Thinking).

When students considered a stranger with whom they disagree, they tended to score the person around 40 – suggesting the person probably formed their opinions based more on external influences. When students considered a stranger with whom they agree, they tended to score the person around 55 – suggesting the person probably formed their opinions based slightly more on internal thinking. This difference might not seem large, but when combined with other statistical considerations, it can be termed "statisically significant."[12]

At a later time, I asked each student, anonymously, to rate their preference for either the democratic or republican political parties. Results indicated that students who strongly favored the democratic party and students who strongly favored the republican party showed the greatest amounts of prejudgment. Students who reported that they were neutral with respect to either political party, or only had a mild preference for either the democratic or republican party, showed less prejudgment.

This makes sense, and it suggests the degree to which we will be narrow-minded and manifest prejudgment will always be a function of how much we care about the issue at hand. For example, the more we care about politics, then the more prejudgment we will manifest when evaluating things related to politics. Or, the more we care about religion, then the more prejudgment we will manifest when evaluating things related to religion.

Several years ago, I made the statement that "being narrow-minded is part of the human condition."[13] And the title of this chapter suggests open-mindedness is an illusion. But there might be an exception. Maybe it is possible to be open-minded. If prejudgment and narrow-mindedness are indeed functions of the degree to which we care about something, then all we need to do to be completely open-minded is "Don't care about anything." Or as Bertrand Russell once stated, "A mind perpetually open will be a mind perceptually vacant."[14] Either way, an unlikely exception.

Chapter 7

I Am Right; You Are Wrong

"The fundamental cause of trouble in the world today is that
the stupid are cocksure while the intelligent are full of doubt."
– Bertrand Russell, *Mortals and Others: American Essays 1931-1935*

Throughout the history of humankind, people have expressed beliefs in certain ideologies – political beliefs, religious beliefs, and philosophical beliefs. And people often express a lot of certainty for those beliefs. In *Being Wrong*, Kathryn Schulz suggests we think otherwise:

> A whole lot of us go through life assuming that we are basically right, basically all the time, about basically everything: about our political and intellectual convictions, our religious and moral beliefs, our assessment of other people, our memories, our grasp of facts. As absurd as it sounds when you stop to think about it, our steady state seems to be one of unconsciously assuming that we are very close to omniscient.[1]

How do we become so convinced about some of our beliefs, especially when other people disagree? And how can we think we are so right, perhaps 100% correct, and then assume others are so wrong? Neurologist Robert Burton suggests it's because "certainty" for any belief is a feeling. It is more of an emotional state as opposed to a logical, reasoned state. He says, "Despite how certainty feels, it is neither a conscious choice nor even a thought process. Certainty and similar states of 'knowing what we know' arise out of involuntary brain mechanisms that, like love or anger, function independently of reason."[2]

Burton then describes research showing that whenever we express certainty for a belief, the pleasure regions of our brains tend to be more active. He refers to such pleasure as a "subliminal cheerleader" that shouts out a gleeful cheer – perhaps, "Hooray, I am right and I know it" – whenever we experience certainty for any of our a beliefs.[3]

In a similar way, Robert Abelson says our beliefs are like possessions. We hold on to them because they make us feel good.[4] In turn, which beliefs make us feel the best? The ones for which we are 100% convinced that we are correct. Schulz adds that "the very word 'believe' comes from an Old English verb meaning 'to hold dear,' which suggests, correctly, that we have a habit of falling in love with our beliefs once we've formed them."[5]

The classic experiment demonstrating that there's a physiological link between experiencing certainty for a belief and feeling good has been conducted by Drew Westen and colleagues at Emory University.[6] Using functional MRI scans, they showed that when participants process information about political beliefs, they tend to show increased MRI activity in lower regions of the brain, specifically the limbic system which is the primary location for emotions. Participants do not show similar increases of activity in the upper regions of the brain, specifically the frontal lobe where higher-order thinking and reasoning occur.

This pattern of results should be expected whenever the information that is presented challenges our political views. That's when we probably feel defensive. Emotions kick in, and rational thought goes to the back burner. But interestingly, the same pattern of results occurs when the information supports our political views. Thus, Westen and colleagues propose that the thought processes behind many of our political beliefs are a kind of motivated reasoning, high on emotion and not nearly as high on rational thought as we would expect. They say it is a "qualitatively distinct" kind of reasoning compared to how we process information for beliefs that we consider less important.[7]

This research and similar studies explain how so many of us become one-sided in the way we deal with politics. Jonathan Haidt elaborates and describes the extent to which such partisanship can occur:

All animal brains are designed to create flashes of pleasure when the animal does something important for its survival, and small pulses of the neurotransmitter dopamine in the ventral striatum (and a few other places) are where these good feelings are manufactured. Heroin and cocaine are addictive because they artificially trigger this dopamine response. Rats who can press a button to deliver electrical stimulation to their reward centers will continue pressing until they collapse from starvation.

And if this is true, then it would explain why extreme partisans are so stubborn, close-minded, and committed to [certain] beliefs . . . Like rats that cannot stop pressing a button, partisans may be simply unable to stop believing [extreme] things. The partisan brain has been reinforced so many times for performing mental contortions that free it from unwanted beliefs. Extreme partisanship may be literally addictive.[8]

Throughout the history of humankind, it probably has always been reinforcing, psychologically, to feel some degree of certainty whenever we make a decision. Can you imagine one of our early ancestors wandering away from the village for a day and then trying to decide which of several routes is best for returning home? If we would not experience any reinforcing quality for trying one route over another route, it would be harder and much more frustrating to eventually make a choice. We would continually be second-guessing ourselves.

In *The Will to Believe*, William James presents a more dramatic example to illustrate the same point. Imagine a man hiking in the Alps and approaching a very deep and dangerous crevasse. It is impossible for the man to hike around the crevasse, and it is impractical for him to think about backtracking. So should he try jumping the crevasse? Probably. But the key question is "How should the man feel about his decision to jump, if he decides to do so?" Moderately certain or very certain? James suggests it is going to be much better for him if he feels very certain about his decision. It will be psychologically rewarding and probably better for his health and safety.[9]

There are researchers who go further and propose that genetics contribute in predisposing us for certain types of beliefs.[10] This is not to suggest that any of our specific beliefs are predetermined. Instead it means that our comfort levels for certain beliefs are genetically predisposed, or our potentials for certain beliefs are genetically set up. As such, we should never expect two different people to somehow end up with the same beliefs even if they were raised in exactly the same way or exposed to the same information. Simply put, we have different brains, and we will always process information in different ways.

As an example, Burton says we should never expect an artist or musician to have the same beliefs – political, religious, or whatever – as a scientist or a mathematician. And in his words, we must give up the wrongheaded idea that "reasonable discourse can establish the superiority of one line of thought over another."[11]

This has implications for how we think about ourselves and how we think about others. In short, our beliefs about various topics and issues are not as superior as we think. They are preferences. And the people with whom we disagree are not as inferior as we think. They are just different. Schulz puts it this way:

> Since we think our own beliefs are based on facts, we conclude that people who disagree with us just haven't been exposed to the right information, and that such exposure would inevitably bring them over to our team. This assumption is extraordinarily widespread. To cite only the most obvious examples, all religious evangelism and a good deal of political activism (especially grassroots activism) is premised on the conviction that you can change people's beliefs by educating them on the issues.[12]

There are two well-established psychological principles that further explain how we become so sure of ourselves regarding our beliefs. The first one is based on our internal desire for cognitive consistency as opposed to inconsistency. Once we simply start to believe something, and perhaps act on the belief, we will have a tendency – consciously or unconsciously – to strengthen the belief for the sake of consistency. The second one is based on our tendency to strengthen beliefs as we spend more and more time with people who think similarly. Consider each in turn.

Cognitive Consistency

There is a fascinating relationship between what we do and what we believe. Most people readily agree that if we have certain beliefs, then those beliefs increase the chances that we might act in corresponding ways. But interestingly, the relationship also goes in the other direction. That is, if we act in certain ways, then those actions will increase the chances that we eventually believe in corresponding ways. David Myers refers to it as one of psychology's "premier lessons," and he suggests, "We are as likely to act ourselves into a way of thinking as to think ourselves into action."[13]

For an example, consider this scenario adapted from one used by Daniel Kahneman:

> Two avid sports fans plan to travel 40 miles to see a basketball game. One of them went to a ticket office, opened her wallet, and actually paid for her ticket. The other fan was given a ticket from a friend who was unable to attend the game. A blizzard is announced for the night of the game. Which of the two ticket holders now thinks her ticket is important, valuable, and not to be wasted?[14]

Most likely, it's the first fan. She did more or invested more, to get her ticket. Psychologically, this is based on an internal desire for what is termed "cognitive consistency."[15] Whenever we perform an action, we have an internal motivation to automatically believe that the action was worth whatever effort we may have exerted. And the more that is exerted, the more we experience this underlying motivation to justify the worthiness of the action. To do otherwise would be psychologically inconsistant and awkward.

This is not limited to physical actions. It includes mental actions. Thus, we not only act ourselves into a way of thinking, but we can "think ourselves into a way of thinking." In doing so, we can foster a sense of ownership in our beliefs. As Dan Ariely suggests, such ownership can become quite extreme:

> Ownership is not limited to material things. It can also apply to points of view. Once we take ownership of an idea – whether it's about politics or sports – what do we do? We love it perhaps more than we should. We prize it more than

it is worth. And most frequently, we have trouble letting go of it because we can't stand the idea of its loss. What are we left with then? An ideology – rigid and unyielding.[16]

Perhaps the clearest demonstration of this actions-to-belief tendency was conducted by Craig Anderson and colleagues at Stanford University.[17] They initially gave participants information about firefighters and asked them to provide reasons why the information might be true. Thus, participants needed to expend mental effort (mental actions) to think about why the information might be true. For half of the participants the information was that risk-takers make the best firefighters. For the other participants the information was that cautious people make the best firefighters. Then after each participant finished thinking about, and writing about, why such people make the best firefighters, the researchers confessed that the information they presented was false. There was no evidence to support either of the claims, that risky or cautious people make the best firefighters.

Will participants discard the beliefs they started to form about firefighters, because they now know that the foundations for the beliefs are false? No, not completely. Later, Anderson and colleagues asked each participant to report what type of person they believed would make the best firefighter. All participants tended to give answers that were consistent with their initial thoughts and actions. The ones who spent time thinking and writing about why risk-takers would make the best firefighters, tended to stick with a corresponding belief – that risk-takers are best. The ones who spent time thinking and writing about why cautious people would make the best firefighters, did likewise. They tended to stick with the belief that cautious firefighters are best.

So the more time and effort we spend entertaining the possibility of a belief, the more we experience an underlying motivation to believe it is true. As the saying goes, "Say it often enough [or think about it often enough], and you'll start to believe it is true." Sigmund Freud once admitted that something like this happened in his own life as he was developing his theory about the importance of the unconscious. He said, "It was only tentatively that I put forward the views I have developed . . . but in the course of time they have gained such a hold upon me that I can no longer think in any other way."[18]

Group Polarization

There's an old adage that "two heads are better than one." Maybe. In this section, I will not argue the overall merits, per se, of "two heads," but instead I describe a psychological tendency that occurs when two or more heads are together. It's a tendency that is magnified if the people who are involved already have similar beliefs or priorities.

In the early 1960s, James Stoner conducted a study at Massachusetts Institute of Technology to identify the tendencies that occur when people serve on committees. Specifically, what happens when you put two or more "heads" together to discuss some issue, weighing the pros and cons, and eventually make a recommendation?[19]

Stoner constructed a variety of scenarios. In each, a protagonist needed to choose between two alternatives with a mix of strengths and weaknesses. For each scenario, Stoner initially had participants work by themselves in considering the scenario and then rate the degree to which they believed one alternative would be a better choice compared to the other. In a second phase, Stoner had participants work in groups to discuss the scenario and its alternatives. In these group settings, he encouraged participants to discuss issues related to each alternative and consider various pros and cons. Then in a third phase, Stoner had participants again work by themselves, as they did in the first phase, to re-consider the scenario. Again, they were to rate the degree to which they believed one alternative would be a better choice compared to the other.

Here is an example. For this scenario, what would you recommend?

> You have a friend who will pursue graduate study in psychology leading to the Ph.D. degree. She has been accepted by University A and University B. University A has a very high reputation. A degree from this university would indicate she is an outstanding scholar, but the standards are so rigorous that only a fraction of its students actually graduate. University B, on the other hand, has a lower reputation, but almost everyone graduates.

Here are the chances your friend would graduate from University A with its high reputation. Check the lowest percentage you consider acceptable for her to enroll at University A, instead of University B.

____There is a 90% chance she would graduate from University A.

____There is a 70% chance she would graduate from University A.

____There is a 50% chance she would graduate from University A.

____There is a 30% chance she would graduate from University A.

____There is a 10% chance she would graduate from University A.[20]

Remember that Stoner had participants respond to such a scenario two times – once before they had the chance to discuss it with other people and once after they had the chance to discuss it with other people. Stoner predicted that after group discussion, most participants would become more cautious in their thinking. In this example, becoming more cautious would be scaling up. (Checking closer to 90% chance for success is considered relatively cautious. Checking closer to 10% chance for success is considered risky and relatively extreme.) Results indicated the opposite. Instead of becoming more cautious, participants tended to become more risky or extreme. They lowered the probabilities for success they considered acceptable for the friend to enroll at the university where she might not succeed.

After Stoner's original research, there have been many studies designed to address what is now called "group polarization." It refers to our tendency to form more extreme opinions after having the opportunity to discuss ideas with other people. The theory is that whenever you have several people together in a group discussing an issue that has different sides, there will almost always be one side that has an initial advantage with more individuals favoring that side. Then, whichever side has the initial advantage, that side will be the direction toward which most individuals slant after group discussion. And over time, with more opportunities to discuss the issue, individuals in the group will tend to slant further in that same direction. Thus, eventually they become even more extreme.

There are two main reasons why this occurs. The first is based on the information that is shared and attained. During a discussion, each person in the group probably hears several things they never heard before; they attain new information. Whichever side of the issue has the initial advantage, then that will be the side that ends up with the most information being shared and attained. Opinions and beliefs slant accordingly.

The second reason is based on attitudes. During a group discussion, it is not only information that is shared. Attitudes also get expressed. For example, when a person joins a discussion about a certain issue, perhaps political or religious, there is a good chance they already have an attitude about which side, of various alternatives, is best. As the discussion progresses, they tend to compare their attitude to that of others. If one side of the issue has an initial advantage, attitude-wise, because more people in the group share essentially the same attitude, then individuals in the group will likely shift bit-by-bit in that direction. In doing so, they would be manifesting an even stronger attitude in the preferred direction. They might even end up envisioning themselves as better people.[21]

Now consider politics and what happens when like-minded people get together. Let's start with an example on the left. Imagine a group of politically liberal-leaning individuals getting together and talking about various issues. They will share information, and most of the information will be supportive of the liberal side. Over time, it is likely that each person will hear several things they did not know before. With that additional information, there will be a tendency to slant further to the left and with increased confidence in what they believe.

Second, imagine a group of right-leaning individuals getting together and talking about various issues. It is likely each person in the group already has a pre-conceived attitude that the conservative side is best. As they interact and subtly compare themselves with each other and those on the other side, each person will have a tendency to slant further to the right. After all, that is the side they consider to be the best, so they would be slanting in the better direction. Over time, each person in the group will probably feel increasingly justified in what they believe. Not only will they envision themselves as correct, but it's likely they will also envision themselves as better, especially when compared to those who have different beliefs.

So in two fundamental ways, what we believe and the certainty with which we believe it, are functions of who we hang around with. When we are with like-minded people, we share information that is mostly supportive of one side, our side, and we insinuate that our side is somehow better and other sides are somehow inferior. As David Brooks says, "People bend their philosophies and their perceptions of reality so they become more and more aligned with members of their political tribe . . . Party affiliation often shapes values, not the other way around."[22]

A Modest Proposal

Researchers like me are enamored with a concept called the *p*-value.[23] Basically, it is an acknowledgement of the *probability* that "I could be wrong." So whenever we make an official statement about research results, we end the statement with a mathematical phrase giving the estimated probability that the statement could be wrong. Research often involves numbers, so the estimated probability is based on how the numbers panned out from statistical calculations.

Researchers also have thresholds for when an outcome or a belief should be stated. In psychology, we almost always adhere to what is termed the 5% rule. It means we should not talk as if a research outcome is worthy of belief, unless the estimated probability for that outcome being wrong is less than 5%. Thus, whenever we are fairly sure that a research outcome is worthy of belief, we end our statements with $p < .05$, which statistically means the probability I could be wrong is less than .05.

Wouldn't it be great if everyone would talk like researchers, ending their statements about beliefs with an acknowledgment that they could be wrong? But instead of acknowledging that the probability is less than .05, it would be better if we would end our statements acknowledging that the probability is greater than .05. Thus, "Here is my belief, and the probability I could be wrong is at least .05."

I submit that this would be a good first step for increasing tolerance in our contentious political environment. When a person is convinced that they are 100% correct about some issue, it clearly justifies their notions that those who disagree are downright wrong and probably inferior in a variety of ways. But if a person acknowledges that they might be wrong, even if only to a small degree, they are then allowing some amount of dignity for those with whom they disagree. As Burton says, "It is in the leap from 99.99999 percent likely to a 100 percent guarantee that we give up tolerance for conflicting opinions, and provide the basis for the fundamentalist's claim to pure and certain knowledge."[24]

Chapter 8

Overvalued Values

"Don't call a person honest just because he or she
never had the chance to steal."
– Yiddish Proverb (Paraphrased)

One of the leading U.S. news events of 2012 occurred when a renowned assistant football coach at the Pennsylvania State University was convicted of sexually molesting numerous boys over a period of years.[1] During the time that this was occurring, there were several people at the university who knew something about what was going on. Several influential leaders acted wrongly. Others who were not as influential simply did not do enough to stop the unfortunate events. For now, consider the ones who were less influential. They knew something about what was going on but did not do enough to protect innocent children from further abuse or potential abuse. Why did they not respond more assertively?

One possible explanation is to accuse these individuals of certain character flaws. But might it be that these people have values, are more virtuous than we think, and indeed care about children? And might they also know that sexual abuse is immoral and a crime? Just because a person has moral values does not guarantee that the values will translate to corresponding behavior in a specific situation. Values tend to be general in nature. Aspects of situations tend to be specific. Unfortunately, we do not make such general-to-specific connections as easily as we think.

The classic study demonstrating the overvalued nature of values was conducted in the late 1920s by a psychologist named Hugh Hartshorne and a theologian named Mark May.[2] They, along with others, were concerned about young people in the United States and their troublesome behaviors.

They teamed up for an extensive study that spanned several years. Hartshorne and May set up situations in which participants had opportunities to either cheat or lie. They then recorded how often such behaviors occurred and what types of young people were more apt to succumb.

One of the things Hartshorne and May had participants do was a creative task called the "Circles Test." During this task, participants are given a sheet of paper that presents nine numbered circles of various sizes. With their eyes open, participants are told to memorize the locations of the circles. Then with their eyes closed, they are to write each circle's number within the boundaries of the corresponding circle. Participants do this with five sets of circles. At the end of the test, they are asked to report how many numbers they placed correctly within the circles. Since there were five sets of nine circles, the total possibility for correct responses is 45. Easy enough. But might participants cheat and not have their eyes completely closed when they do this test? Or, might they lie when reporting their results?

This *Circles Test* had been used before with many people who were blindfolded. So Hartshorne and May knew that the test was much harder than people realize, and they knew it was almost impossible for a person who actually had their eyes closed to get more than 23 correct over the five trials. To do so, would be a one in 1,000 occurrence. Thus, if any participant reported that they placed more than 23 numbers correctly without peeking, Hartshorne and May assumed that they had either cheated or they were lying.

That is exactly what most of the participants did, cheat or lie. However, almost all of the participants could describe how and why such behaviors are wrong. Thus, they indicated that they had moral values, but they succumbed nonetheless. Even the participants who appeared to be the most upstanding based on various religious affiliations, tended to cheat or lie to the same degree as those who appeared to have lower moral values. This prompted Hartshorne and May to suggest that adults should spend less time emphasizing general themes when they talk with teenagers about values. Instead they should spend more time talking about how specific temptations might occur in kids' lives and discuss what responses might be best.

Apparently the National Basketball Association adheres to Hartshorne and May's advice. Over the years, the NBA has had an unflattering reputation because too many of its players sired children out of wedlock. So to better prepare young players to deal with the temptations that come with having a lot of money and traveling in various cities, the NBA requires all new players to attend so-called "Rookie Camps."[3]

During parts of these camps, counselors guide the players in role-playing situations. Specific situations are staged so the young players can get a feel for how various temptations might occur in their professional lives. The counselors also talk with the players about what responses might be best and why. This is basically the same as Hartshorne and May suggested years ago.

Back to the scandalous activity at Penn State University. In no way am I condoning the behavior of people who knew something about the possible sexual abuse of children yet did nothing or very little. Instead, I am emphasizing that having beliefs about moral values only goes so far. Values tend to be general in nature. Behaviors occur in specific situations.

In *Blind Spots: Why We Fail to Do What's Right*, Max Brazerman and Ann Tenbrunsel say that even though a person has upright values, it is still hard for the person to truly know how they might respond in a specific situation. Brazerman and Tenbrunsel suggest that thinking about values and how they might apply in a specific situation is like overlooking a forest from a hillside. But being in a specific situation in which the values might apply is like actually navigating the forest and dealing with individual trees. It's quite different. Brazerman and Tenbrunsel put it this way:

> When we think about our future behavior, it is difficult to anticipate the actual situation we will face. General principles and attitudes drive our predictions; we see the forest but not the trees. As the situation approaches, however, we begin to see the trees, and the forest disappears. Our behavior is driven by details, not abstract principles.[4]

Ironically, one of the clearest research demonstrations of how values do not necessarily translate to behavior in a specific situation was conducted at Penn State University by Janet Swim and Lauri Hyers.[5] During the first part of their research, Swim and Hyers surveyed female students at Penn State and asked what they would do if someone made a crude, sexist statement in their presence. Overlooking the forest of life, about 50% of those women confidently reported that they would challenge the inappropriate statement, presumably because it violated something about their values.

During the second part of this research, Swim and Hyers actually staged a situation in which such a crude statement occurred. They recruited other female college students at Penn State to participate in small group discussions. It was assumed that these women had essentially the same values as those surveyed. The other members of the upcoming discussion groups were confederates of the researchers, one of whom was a male student. During the discussions, the male student was told to make several derogatory sexist statements. Results indicated that when these statements occurred (as participants actually navigated the forest of life), only 16% did anything to challenge the statements, compared to the estimated 50% who were confident that they would stand up for their values.

Environmental Cues

The main reason that the link between moral values and subsequent behavior is weak is because cues in the environment are so important in setting up behavior. General concepts such as "love each other, be honest, do not steal, and show compassion," sound great. But by themselves, they rarely specify how and when they should occur, or what aspects of a situation could be used to prime an appropriate response.

A set of studies I conducted at the University of West Alabama is supportive. In the first study, I teamed up with a student named Greg Love.[6] We wanted to evaluate how easy it might be for religious participants to apply something about their religious priorities in a setting without obvious religious cues. Specifically, would it be easy for very religious participants, Christians in particular, to apply important information from their religious beliefs if given an opportunity to do so in a General Psychology class?

We visited several General Psychology classes and asked the students to take five minutes and think about what they considered to be the "three greatest events in the history of the world." Eventually they were to list the events in any order. At the University of West Alabama we knew that about 90% of the students would be Christians and a good percentage of those would be highly-committed Christians. We wanted to know how many of the students who are highly committed to the teachings of Christianity would list something about the significance of Jesus, or anything else in the Bible, among their top three greatest events, irrespective of how they interpret the word "greatest" – as miraculous or influential.

Results indicated that only 19% of the Christian participants who reported high levels of commitment to the teachings of Christianity identified anything from the Bible, let alone anything about Jesus. When we asked these participants if they believed something like the biblical accounts of the resurrection of Jesus or perhaps the virgin birth of Jesus should be included among the top three events in the history of the world, many said "Yes." But when we asked the 81% who did not identify anything from the Bible, why they did not list anything about Jesus, many responded, "I didn't think of it."

We surmised that the reason so many highly-committed Christians did not think of important aspects of their religious beliefs in this situation is because religious priorities, like values, are not easily applied in specific situations unless there are appropriate environmental cues. Whether General Psychology classes have any appropriate cues for religious beliefs can be debated. Certainly they do not have obvious cues for such beliefs.

Two years after this initial study, I conducted a follow-up experiment to see if I could cue in religious beliefs for religious participants using subliminal perception. I used a perceive-and-respond task similar to that of Patricia Devine described in chapter 4.[7]

First, I had participants sit at a computer station and perform the perceive-and-respond task. They simply needed to press a left or right key on the computer's keyboard to indicate whether a flash of letters (lasting two tenths of a second) appeared to the left or to the right. During that task, half of the participants were subliminally exposed to words such as *church, bible, sermon, and heaven.* The other participants were not exposed to such church-related words. Then immediately after the perceive-and-respond task, all participants were asked, while still sitting at the computer, to list what they believed to be the *three greatest events* in the history of the world.

Among the participants who reported high commitment to Christianity and received subliminal exposure to the religious words, about 48% listed an event from the Bible among the *three greatest events* in history. And almost all of those events included something about Jesus. Among the participants who reported high commitment to Christianity but did not receive exposure to the religious words, only 20% listed a biblical event. Note that the 20% essentially replicates the 19% from the original research with Greg Love.

So presenting religious information subliminally can indeed serve as an environmental cue to help religious individuals tap into their religious priorities, thus increasing the chances that they will respond accordingly.

This suggests it might also be possible to prime something about moral values in the same way. An experiment conducted by Nina Mazar and colleagues at the University of California, Los Angeles, is supportive, although they did not use subliminal perception.[8]

Mazar and colleagues set up a situation in which a group of college students had opportunities to cheat or lie, similar to the Hartshorne and May research described at the beginning of this chapter. Specifically, they had two groups of college students perform a math-related task for five minutes. Participants were given sheets of paper with various numbers listed. As quickly as possible, they were to identify and write down as many pairs of numbers they could find that added to a pre-determined amount.

After completing the task, one group of participants was told to simply hand over their answer sheets to the experimenter for scoring. The other group, however, was told to score their own sheets, then tear up their sheets, and tell the experimenter how many pairs they found. So the second group had an opportunity to cheat or lie, and as expected, they did. They reported superior performance compared to the group that could not have cheated or lied.

There's more. Before each group started this part of the experiment, Mazar and colleagues had participants do one of two things. Half of the participants in each group were asked to recall and list up to 10 books they remembered reading in high school. The other half of participants for each group were asked to recall and list as many of the 10 commandments from the Bible that they could remember. Whether these participants were religious or not, the researchers assumed that the attempts to recall this information primed something related to moral values, irrespective of how many commandments they ended up recalling.

Perhaps the possibility of moral values affecting subsequent behavior can be improved, if the values are primed. For all the participants who had the opportunity to cheat or lie, the half that did not spend time trying to recall the 10 commandments cheated or lied 33% more often than the half that spent time trying to recall the 10 commandments. Thus, time spent thinking about moral values, in this case the 10 commandments, increased the chances of value-appropriate behavior, at least in the short term.

It is likely that all the participants in this research had moral values and believed that cheating and lying are wrong. But having such values that are presumably general in nature, does not guarantee corresponding behavior when temptations occur in specific situations. As Dan Ariely suggests, of course "we care about honesty and we want to be honest. The problem is that our internal honesty monitor is [not always] active."[9] That does not mean we will necessarily be dishonest in a given situation. But it also doesn't mean we should readily assume that we will always be honest in a given situation.

Max Brazerman and Ann Tenbrunsel go further. They suggest that we rarely learn from our lapses in moral judgment:

> Ample evidence suggests that people who, in the abstract, believe they are honest and would never cheat, do in fact cheat when given such an easy, unverifiable opportunity to do so. These people aren't likely to factor this type of cheating into their assessments of their ethical character; instead, they leave the experiment with their positive self-image intact.[10]

Most likely we will always envision ourselves as morally upright, very good, and among the best people in the world.

The Perception of Time

The subliminal perception experiment I conducted and the experiment by Mazar and colleagues demonstrate that providing environmental cues, either via subliminal perception or instructions to think about something, can indeed increase the chances of a religious or moral response. This too has limitations if participants feel constrained by yet another environmental factor – time or the perception of time.

For those of us who still think that our wonderful selves, full of moral values, will always step up and do the right thing no matter what the situation is, consider an experiment with seminary students at Princeton University. Of all people, seminary students should be among the most likely to step up and apply their values in all situations, especially if primed.[11]

Researchers John Darley and Daniel Batson informed their participants (seminary students) that they were supposed to give a short talk in another building on campus at Princeton University. They told them that there would be some scheduling or timing issues, because the talk depended on the availability and involvement of other people. Half of the participants were told that their talk was going to be about the "Parable of the Good Samaritan," a story in the Bible in which a person who was least expected to help a stranger in need, indeed stepped up and did so.[12] The other half were told that their talk was going to be about "career-related opportunities" in ministry.

With respect to the timing issues, some of the participants were told that they were already late for the talk. They were told that the other people who were involved were already waiting for them. In contrast, some participants were told that they had plenty of time, because the other people who were involved would not be ready for the talk until later.

Then, each participant was instructed to start walking to the campus building where the talk was going to be given. What the participants did not realize is that the researchers staged a needy situation along the way. They arranged to have an actor positioned along the pathway where the participant was walking. The actor was dressed rather shabbily, and as the participant approached, the actor started groaning, coughing, and feigning discomfort. So who might be most likely to stop and offer help? Will it be the seminary students who are thinking about the *Good Samaritan* (since that is what their talk will be about) and believe they are already *running late?* Will it be the seminary students who are thinking about the *Good Samaritan* and believe they have *plenty of time?* Will it be the seminary students who are thinking about *career-related information* (since that is what their talk will be about) and believe they are already *running late?* Or, will it be the seminary students who are thinking about *career-related information* and believe they have *plenty of time?*

Results indicated that what matters most is time, or the perception of time, irrespective of what the participants were currently thinking about. Both groups of participants that believed they had plenty of time were significantly more likely to act in a *Good Samaritan* way by stopping and offering help to the struggling actor, compared to both groups that believed they were running late. The two groups of participants that were thinking about the *Good Samaritan* story, only tended to stop and offer help at about the same rate as the two groups that were thinking about *career-related information.*

Thus, even when moral values are primed and we are induced to think about them, there is still no guarantee that the values will manifest themselves when an appropriate situation occurs. When we feel busy, rushed, or constrained by time, there is less chance the values will show up, again suggesting that general principles by themselves are overrated and overvalued.

Additional Remarks

I acknowledge that the statement "values are overrated and overvalued" seems harsh. This does not mean they are not important – just not as important as we think.

We all want to believe that our values and good intentions will make a difference, and for the better. But evidence suggests otherwise. There is hope, however. Just as Hartshorne and May proposed in the 1920s, we must take time to consider exactly how our values might be challenged in specific situations. Then too, we must consider what responses are possible and why some responses would be better, or more consistent with our values, than other possibilities.

Peter Gollwitzer and his collaborators are more specific. They propose that values mostly reside at the conscious level of awareness. But our everyday behavior, which is often routine in nature, tends to be guided by processes at the unconscious level. Thus, we need to make the conscious, unconscious.[13]

To do so, Gollwitzer and colleagues propose that we spend more time imagining exactly how our values might influence our responses in specific situations. We should imagine the values *in action*. In doing so, we will start to form what they refer to as "if-then plans" within our unconscious networks of cognitive associations. And with such "if-then plans" in place, environmental cues will have the best chance possible to prime appropriate behavior. Better yet, do not stop at imagining the plans. Put them into action.

Chapter 9

The Naïve Notion That
"I Could Never Hurt Anyone"

"Most of us dramatically underestimate the degree to which
our behavior is affected by incentives and other situational factors."
– Max Brazerman and Ann Tenbrunsel, *Blind Spots*

I was raised in a religious environment where one of the main emphases was
that a person should never willingly and knowingly inflict physical harm on
anyone else. We considered ourselves to be "pacifists." Everyone probably
has a threshold for when they might physically hurt someone else. For pacifists, that threshold tends to be more stringent. That doesn't mean it could
never happen.

For most of my life, I was convinced that I could never physically hurt
anyone else, even if provoked. Is this true? I remember talking as if it were.
Now I know it's probably not. There is too much evidence to indicate that all
of us are not only capable of very negative, hurtful behavior, but we would
probably do so, if the right situation occurs. To believe otherwise is naïve at
best. Values and good intentions are nice, but as described in chapter 8, they
have less influence over what we do than we think.

Personal Characteristics versus Situational Influences

One of the most profound concepts in psychology, usually attributed to Kurt
Lewin, is that behavior is a function of two things. First, behavior, in part,
comes from the person who actually does the behavior. Here behavior is
considered to be a function of a person's disposition or personal characteristics. But behavior can also come from the environment. Here behavior is

considered to be a function of aspects of the situation a person is experiencing. These personal characteristics and situational influences work in combination. For those with a mathematical mind, it can be stated as "Behavior $= f$ (Person, Situation)," where f means "a function of."[1]

Even though behavior comes from the combination of personal characteristics and situational influences, we have a tendency to focus on only one of the two. When it comes to explaining the behavior of other people, especially the negative behavior of other people, we usually focus on the personal characteristics. The reason is because it is much easier to speculate about the personal characteristics of another person as opposed to trying to understand the specific situation they might have experienced.

Many textbooks in psychology refer to this tendency – to readily focus on personal characteristics, as opposed to situational influences – as the "fundamental attribution error."[2] This suggests focusing on personal characteristics is a mistake and something to be avoided. But it does not represent a mistake per se. For example, if you were to observe someone falling at the bottom of a stairway, you are likely to think that the person is klutzy. That's the easy attribution tendency – explain the person's behavior, in this case falling, by focusing on personal characteristics as opposed to spending time and energy to think about the situational influences that might have occurred. But you might be right. There are some people who are klutzy. On the other hand, you might be wrong. Perhaps, there is something slippery on the steps.

The point is that if you continue to readily attribute behavior to personal characteristics as opposed to situational influences, in the long run, you are likely to be wrong as often as right, if not more. Also, it's unfair, especially when you are evaluating other people. For example, imagine what would happen if you were the one who fell at the bottom of a stairway. If you are like most of us, you will probably consider what might be wrong with the steps or stairway. You are more apt to avoid or at least minimize the "klutzy person" attribution when it happens to you. Thus, when someone else does something negative, "woe unto them." When you do the same thing, situational excuses abound.

Stanley Milgram's Classic Research

In the 1960s, Stanley Milgram, a researcher at Yale University, conducted what is probably the most famous and controversial set of experiments in the history of psychology. He demonstrated that good people, like most of us consider ourselves to be, will knowingly harm someone else, physically, without provocation, if a certain situation occurs.[3]

Milgram was fascinated with the very negative behavior of several people involved in the tragic events of the Holocaust in the early 1900s. In particular, he was fascinated with the behavior of Adolf Eichmann who worked in the Nazi regime during World War II. Eichmann personally organized the deportation and execution of over a million Jewish people.[4] Part of his job was to decide who gets to live, at least for the moment, and who should die. Killing innocent people or making decisions about killing innocent people . . . It is extremely negative behavior. But does that guarantee that Adolf Eichmann was a bad person?

Milgram wasn't convinced. Indeed, what Eichmann did was bad, and it is easy to assume that he had all sorts of personal character flaws. But Milgram wondered if it was possible that bad behavior, including extremely bad behavior, could actually come from a good person caught-up in a very difficult situation. Or, is it possible that extremely bad behavior could be a function of a good person in a negative and very powerful situation?

Neither I nor Stanley Milgram is supporting or justifying Adolf Eichmann's behavior – his involvement in the deaths of many innocent people. Eichmann was found guilty of crimes against humanity and eventually executed, hanged by the neck in 1962. He bears responsibility for his behavior, irrespective of whether or not he might have been a good person with many positive personal characteristics, as Milgram surmised.

In a series of 19 experiments with about 600 participants, Milgram demonstrated that people who do not believe in physically hurting others will probably do so without provocation if certain aspects of a situation are presented. In Milgram's experiments, participants were led to believe that they were delivering electrical shocks to another person as part of a teaching-and-learning experiment. The other person was always a male actor who appeared to be an innocent participant in the research. He simply pretended to be receiving shocks. Sometimes he would gasp. Sometimes he would yell to feign a response to pain. No shocks were ever given to this person, but the real participant in the research was led to believe it was happening and the innocent person was actually being hurt. So the experiment was not about teaching-and-learning. It was about the degree to which a real participant would continue to obey the experimental procedures and deliver what appeared to be painful electric shocks to another person.

When participants showed up for Milgram's research, after agreeing to do so, everything was staged so the actor would show up at the same time, appearing to be another participant. The experimenter then explained that one person would need to serve as the teacher and the other would need to be the learner, exactly what is needed for an ostensibly teacher-and-learner investigation. The experimenter conducted a rigged form of drawing straws to give the impression that the two persons were being randomly assigned to the teacher and learner roles. The real participant was always guaranteed to be the teacher. The actor would always be the learner.

Then the experimenter escorted the actor-learner to a room to be strapped into a chair, with the participant-teacher watching. The participant-teacher was taken to a nearby room with a desk and an impressive machine called a shock generator. The machine had 30 switches to deliver shocks between 15 volts to 450 volts, in 15 volt increments. The higher levels of shocks even had labels like "Danger: Severe Shock." During the experiment, the teacher was to read combinations of words, and the learner was to eventually learn the combinations. Whenever the learner made a mistake, he was supposed to receive an electric shock, presumably to facilitate learning. The first shocks were light, but the intensity was to be increased with each mistake.

Now the experiment begins. Imagine you are in this situation as the teacher-participant. For the first few mistakes, and shocks, the actor-learner does not express any pain. But eventually, he starts to gasp or say "Ouch." Later, he starts to yell or scream in pain and occasionally, he pleads to be unstrapped and left out of the experiment. At what point, will you, the teacher, refuse to continue? If you are like most teacher-participants, you will often balk, express frustration, and even say you want to stop. But that doesn't mean you will stop. The experimenter explains that he will take responsibility for whatever danger the learner might be experiencing, so you continue to deliver electric shocks, increasing the voltage each time.

Stanley Milgram and other psychologists were surprised at the results of the initial experiments. Virtually all of the teacher-participants – good people, like you and me – willingly and knowingly administered what they believed to be painful electric shocks to the actor-learner. Furthermore, about 65% of the teacher-participants continued to do so to the end of the experiment, believing they were delivering very intense 450 volt shocks to the other person.[5]

Milgram conducted a variety of subsequent experiments. In each, he altered certain aspects of the situation, and these aspects tended to either increase or decrease the amount of pressure the teacher-participants experienced. The pattern of results varied somewhat. But the overall conclusion stayed the same. In this situation, almost all good people will administer painful shocks to another person. Some good people will do so less often. Most good people will do so to the max.

Can these results be trusted? The original experiments took place in the 1960s and only in the United States. Would the pattern of results hold up if the research was conducted today or in other countries? In 2006, several of the experiments were replicated at Santa Clara University in California, and variations have been conducted in several other countries on four different continents.[6] In total, there have been about 3,000 participants involved in this kind of research.[7] Also, the research has been replicated as part of a reality television series in England. (Conduct a *YouTube* search with Stanley Milgram's name, and you can watch replications.) Overall, the pattern of results has always been the same.[8] So yes, Milgram's results appear to be very trustworthy and applicable to all of us. To believe otherwise is simply wishful thinking.

Should the results be surprising? Only to someone who continues to adhere to the easy attribution – the presumed fundamental attribution error – that behaviors come from personal characteristics of the person who is involved in the situation. Since participants' behaviors in Milgram's research were very negative, such an individual would need to believe that virtually all of Milgram's participants were bad people who had no qualms about hurting another person. Milgram's results should not be surprising to anyone who understands that behavior can be strongly influenced by aspects of a situation, which was Milgram's initial intrigue in the life and death of Adolph Eichmann.

So what aspects of Milgram's experimental situation were powerful and help to explain how very good people can end up doing very bad things? There are two that stand out. First, good people agreed to participate and everything seemed innocent as the experiment began. The insidious parts of the experiment occurred later and progressed in small steps. Second, there were time constraints for the experiment, so everything needed to progress at a steady pace, if not a fast pace. Consider each, in turn.

Cognitive Consistency

In chapter 7, I described how the relationship between actions and our corresponding beliefs can go both ways. Beliefs can affect actions, but actions can also affect beliefs. The actions-to-beliefs direction is based on our internal motivation for cognitive consistency.[9] Once we begin to do something, we experience an unconscious desire to justify it, to believe in its value, and to continue doing it. To do otherwise would be inconsistent and psychologically awkward.

An interesting demonstration was conducted at a horse racetrack in British Columbia.[10] Researchers asked various people to rate the level of confidence they had in believing that the horse they were betting on would win the upcoming race. For half of the participants, the researchers asked *just before* the participants actually placed their bets. For the other half, the researchers asked *just after* they placed their bets. Participants who were asked to rate the level of confidence they had in their beliefs, *after* they took the action of investing their money, tended to express higher levels of confidence, compared to the participants who were asked *before* they took that action. So the action of committing money to a wager tended to increase levels of confidence in the horses the participants chose.

Now consider how this principle applies in Stanley Milgram's research. In his research, participants first agreed to participate. Second, they showed up for the experiment. Third, they went through the drawing-straws charade, and they considered it legitimate. Fourth, they watched the actor-participant get strapped into his chair. Fifth, they paid close attention as the "how to be a teacher" instructions were given. Sixth, they started presenting word combinations and giving a few mild shocks for mistakes. Even at this point, it appeared that no one was getting hurt, so everything seemed okay. But also at this point and earlier points, they are clearly invested in the experimental procedure. To continue would be consistent. To turn back at any point would be inconsistent and psychologically awkward. And the further they go with this procedure, the more awkward it will be to stop and quit.

From your perspective what will happen once the actor-learner expresses pain for the first time, in response to you flipping a switch for an incorrect answer? Do you quit the experiment, because you don't believe in hurting anyone? Or do you, like almost everyone else who has experienced this situation, continue, perhaps rationalizing that he's probably okay. The expression of pain wasn't too loud. Also, this experiment is being conducted at a very prestigious university. You are confident that they know what they are doing with respect to exposing anyone to serious pain.

Now consider a few more flips of switches and a few more expressions of pain, even louder, coming from the actor-learner. What do you do? And what do you do if the actor-learner clearly states that he wants to stop the research? Perhaps at this point, the experimenter sitting at another desk in your room reminds you that he will take full responsibility for anything that happens to the learner. You and your actions are well-invested in this research and its procedure. In a very important way, a way based on your internal need for consistency, it might be easier to take one more step, a small step, in this wrong direction than to turn back and quit the experiment. Your well-intentioned values about never hurting anyone might be strong, but not strong enough in this situation.

Details and Pace

A second reason why Stanley Milgram's experimental situation is so powerful is that all the experiments were designed to fit into a certain period of time, usually one hour. Whenever there was a lull in how the experiment was progressing, it's likely the participant would be encouraged to "continue please" without long delays. Also, at the beginning of the experiment there were a lot of experimental details to which the participants needed to pay attention. And during the experiment, they needed to continue to focus on certain details about what was going on. In short, they never had much time or energy to consciously reflect on all that was happening.

What if Milgram would have designed an experiment in which participants were required to take a break? Maybe after delivering a shock around 150 volts, the experimenter would say, "Let's take a 15 minute break. Stand up, take a walk down the hallway, maybe get a drink of water, and come back in 15 minutes. Then we will continue the experiment." Such an experiment was never done. If it were, I believe a high majority of participants, those good people who do not believe in hurting others, would have quit the experiment. But when there are many things to pay attention to and you must keep up with a relatively fast pace, it's a lot harder to end up doing the right thing.

Summary

Behavior is a function of two things – the personal characteristics of the person who is involved and aspects of the situation. But we tend to readily explain behavior by only focusing on the personal characteristics of whoever is involved. It's what some researchers refer to as the "fundamental attribution error," suggesting it's a mistake and should be avoided. It might not always be a mistake, but it is a rather lazy way of thinking. Situations can be much more influential than we realize and are willing to admit. Thus, we should be increasingly careful about faulting others when they behave in less than optimal ways. We should also be a bit more careful about flattering ourselves whenever we behave in very good ways. Aspects of the situation might have contributed to our behavior much more than we realize.

Furthermore, we should be careful about thinking that we would always step up and do the right thing in a difficult situation. Stanley Milgram's 19 experiments, along with a host of replications, have demonstrated that virtually all of us would physically hurt someone else, willingly and knowingly, if the right, or should I say wrong situation occurred. To believe otherwise is wishful thinking and naive. Sociologist Eric Silver isn't quite as kind. He suggests we're "full of crap" or full of wrongheaded thinking whenever we believe in our own individual exceptionalism in the face of such convincing evidence.[11]

Chapter 10

The Do-Gooder's Dilemma

"All variants of voluntary effort – cognitive, emotional, or physical –
draw at least partly on a shared pool of mental energy."
– Daniel Kahneman, *Thinking, Fast and Slow*

Many researchers propose that humans have an internal desire to be good
and do good.[1] Some refer to it as an internal desire to establish moral self-
worth. It is essentially the same as a conscience, or Sigmund Freud's concept
of a superego. But if we have an internal desire to be good and do good, then
how good do we need to be? Or, how much good do we need to do?

Many researchers also propose that the psychological resources we
have for being good or even desiring to be good are limited in nature.[2] Thus,
as we expend resources to pursue goodness in one area of our lives, we will
have fewer resources available for pursuing goodness in other areas. There's
always a tradeoff. So while we think we want to be very good in many different ways, in actuality it is not possible.

In the early 1980s, William Catton wrote an influential book entitled
Overshoot. It was a wake-up call about how we need to be careful about consuming, and over consuming, the earth's natural resources. Resources are
limited, yet our consumption suggests we believe they are unlimited. Two
concepts follow. First, "carrying capacity" refers to the extent to which the
earth can actually handle our consumption of resources. Second, the "cornucopian myth" refers to our overly optimistic belief that these resources
will always exist, abundantly.[3]

But if the earth's physical resources are limited, yet we act as if they are
not, might similar concepts occur in the same way for our psychological
resources? Something is limited with respect to our psychological resources.

The resources that we have available for genuinely caring about important things in life could be considered as "caring capacity." Yet we maintain overly optimistic beliefs that these resources are unlimited. Many of us think that we will always be capable of genuinely caring about important matters in abundance. Thus, a new kind of "cornucopian myth."

Certainly, there are many worthy needs around the world that any one person could care about and desire to improve, and it seems obvious that there will always be a limit to what any one person could physically do. That's because resources like time and money are limited. As a person allocates more of those resources to one concern, then by necessity, less will be available for other concerns. There is always a tradeoff.

For example, imagine the wealthiest person in the world trying to do it all when it comes to being good. Theoretically, the person could start by evenly distributing a moderate amount of time, money, or other physical resources to every needy situation in the world. But as the person increases what they give to one needy situation, then by necessity, there will be less available for what they can give to other situations. It is true that they could almost always give a little bit more to help a few needy situations or a little bit more to help all situations. Eventually, this will create a strain on their resources, and at some point, the resources will be depleted, and they will not be able to do anything else.

Now consider a similar kind of tradeoff for psychological resources such as personal interest and concern. Imagine the most compassionate person in the world trying to care about every needy situation. Theoretically, the person could evenly distribute a moderate amount of interest and concern for each situation. But as they increase psychological resources for one needy situation, by necessity, less will be available for other situations. It is true that they could almost always care a little bit more for a few needy situations or a little bit more for all situations. Eventually, this will create a strain, and at some point the psychological resources will be depleted, and they will not be able to care any more.

There are several researchers who have coined creative terms for the idea that psychological resources can be consumed and over-consumed as described above – psychology's version of Catton's *Overshoot*. Roy Baumeister refers to it as "ego depletion," and Kathleen Vohs describes the "hangover effect" that can occur when we over-extend ourselves by caring too much for one thing and not having much left for anything else.[4] James

Shah goes further. He suggests that once we choose something to really care about, we not only expend resources to care about the concern, but also to make sure other concerns do not interfere. He refers to it as "goal shielding."[5] It's as if we unconsciously go out of our way to avoid dealing with any additional concerns whenever we have something major to care about.

However all this occurs, it presents a "dilemma" for any well-intentioned person who desires to do good. Simply put, there are not only limits to what we can do, but also limits to what we can care about doing – limits to our *caring capacity*. Thus, we must make choices about what we will care about. To believe otherwise represents a new kind of *cornucopian myth*.

Moral Self-Worth, Credentials, and Licensing

There's more. There is also research to indicate that once we reach a certain point in doing good, not based on a cognitive limit per se, we still have a tendency to slack off because we have already established some amount of moral credibility. The basic theory is that all of us have an internal desire for moral self-worth, something akin to a conscience. As a result we genuinely want to do some good things in our lives and establish, as researchers say, "moral credentials." But we do not need to overdo it. After establishing enough credentials, we can either slack off or perhaps feel entitled to do something negative.[6]

Establishing *moral credentials* can be done in a variety of ways. The most obvious is through behavior – "do good." But we can also establish our moral credentials through our talk – "say the right things." Some researchers have even suggested that we can do it through our political affiliations.[7] For example, we might consider ourselves to have high moral credibility simply because we adhere to a political ideology or support certain political issues.[8]

As an example, consider, Ron Sider's *The Scandal of the Evangelical Conscience*. In it, Sider presents a scathing account about how many Christians who adhere to the *religious right*, do not appear to be applying their moral standards to their own day-to-day lives. Instead of caring for the poor and disenfranchised as much as you would expect, they appear to be focused on their own self-interests. He presents quite a bit of evidence to indicate that they are just as materialistic as everyone else.[9]

Why does this occur? One plausible reason is their involvement in politics. Many people on the *religious right* overtly moralize about political issues such as abortion. It's likely that such activity helps them establish moral credentials to the point where they do not feel they need to do much more. It frees them from needing to be as good in other areas of their lives.

On the flip side consider a critique of the *secular left*. In *Who Really Cares*, Arthur Brooks presents an equally scathing account about how many people who adhere to the *secular left* do not show as much personal concern for the poor and disenfranchised as you would expect. Politically, they vote in ways that suggest they care about the poor and disenfranchised, but when it comes to personal giving, they do less than people who do not vote in similar ways. Brooks presents quite a bit of evidence to indicate that they contribute less money to organizations that help those in need and they spend less time volunteering with such organizations.[10]

Why does this occur? Again, one plausible reason is their involvement in politics. It is likely that voting in ways that support certain moral causes helps them establish enough moral credentials so that it frees them from needing to do anything else to justify their goodness. (Those on the *secular right* and *religious left* can be critiqued in the same way.)

Some researchers have identified more specific ways in which political involvements can reduce a person's motivation to be good in other ways. Sonya Sachdeva and colleagues suggest that when a person participates in a morally-charged political event, perhaps a rally for some cause, it reduces the chances that the person will subsequently "donate blood."[11] Angela Krumm and Alexandria Corning go further. They propose that when a person does something overly good to over-credential themselves morally, they can feel "licensed" to do something negative. The example they give is that if a person develops a solid reputation for being an advocate for some marginalized group of people, perhaps an ethnic group or socio-economic group, they might be more likely (compared to others) to make derogatory comments about the group.[12]

Again, all this presents a dilemma for anyone who wants to do good. To some extent, we must choose how we want to be good. It is not simply a matter of doing good, and more good, and more good, in all areas of our lives and in all ways we can imagine. At some point, it takes a toll, and we slack off whether we realize it or not.

I can relate. During the winter months in Pennsylvania, I volunteer quite a bit with a temporary shelter program for homeless women and children. But I have started noticing that when I am busiest with the shelter, I am rather careless in my recycling efforts, at both my office and in our home. My do-gooding with the homeless shelter is more than enough to satisfy my overall moral self-worth. Thus, I feel credentialed and even licensed to back off in other areas of my life. With that said, I vow to not let my recycling efforts slide next winter. It remains to be seen whether or not something else related to my presumed goodness, takes a hit.

Supportive Research

There are a variety of studies that have demonstrated how moral *credentialing* and *licensing* operate. They usually involve two phases. First, participants are given an opportunity to express themselves morally, thus establishing credentials. Then during a second phase, the participants may or may not step up to the proverbial plate and manifest additional goodness. If they feel fully credentialed, morally, in the first phase, then they will be less likely to manifest additional goodness in the second phase. Consider three studies.

In an experiment conducted by Sachdeva and colleagues at Northwestern University, participants were initially given nine words to copy and think about.[13] Then each participant was to write a personal story about themselves using all nine words. They were specifically instructed to visualize how each word might be relevant to their lives as they write. For one group of participants, the words were morally positive characteristics such as *kind, generous, and caring*. For another group, the words were morally negative characteristics such as *selfish, greedy, and mean*. For a third group of participants, the words were morally neutral concepts such as *house, keys, and book*. Presumably, it is the participants in the first group who will feel an increase in moral credentialing as they write their personal story.

At the end of the experiment, and following an intermediate phase that was unrelated to the writing task, Sachdeva and colleagues informed all participants that the psychology department was trying to promote awareness for various social issues among all its students. It was portrayed as unrelated to the experiment that participants just completed. Specifically, participants were told that if they wanted to, they could choose a charity and contribute money to the charity as part of this social awareness campaign. But for now, they only needed to make a pledge up to a maximum of $10.00. The researchers would contact them later to follow up with the actual contribution.

Participants who wrote a personal story using morally neutral words pledged an average of $2.71. Participants who wrote a personal story using morally negative words such as *selfish, greedy, and mean,* pledged an average of $5.30. It appears these participants increased their desire to give based on a need to compensate for the moral deficiencies they had just experienced. But how about the participants who had recently increased their moral credentials by writing a personal story while focusing on and using words like *kind, generous, and caring*? They pledged an average of only $1.07 to the charity of their choice. Apparently they felt morally credentialed and sufficient, so there was no need to do more.

In an experiment conducted by Uzma Khan and Ravi Dhar at Yale University, college students participated in two apparently unrelated tasks.[14] For the first task, half of the participants were asked to imagine that they had volunteered for three hours a week helping with one of two community service projects. One project was teaching children at a homeless shelter, and one was working to improve the local environment. Participants chose which volunteer effort they would consider, and then they described how they imagined it would be to follow through with the effort. The other half of the participants did not need to perform this task.

For the second task, all participants were told to imagine that they were shopping at a mall where there were sales on a variety of items. They were asked to also imagine having $50 to spend and needing to choose between purchasing a pair of designer jeans marked down to $50 and a vacuum cleaner on sale for $50. What is the likelihood that participants will choose to purchase the designer jeans, a fairly self-indulgent luxury item, as opposed to the vacuum cleaner, a more practical necessity item?

Results indicated that the participants who had imagined themselves volunteering for three hours per week for a charitable cause were twice as likely to choose the designer jeans as participants who did not imagine themselves volunteering for such a worthy cause. After conducting four additional experiments yielding similar results, Khan and Dhar conclude that people often show "preferences for luxury options after a prior decision makes them appear virtuous."[15] Again, performing an action that seems to help us establish our moral credentials, in turn, tends to reduce a kind of need to continue doing good, and in some cases, it even provides a license to indulge ourselves more than we would otherwise.

In both of the experiments described so far, participants failed to pledge money or consider spending money in virtuous ways after envisioning themselves doing moral actions. But the moral issues participants dealt with in the two phases were never the same. Perhaps if the issues were, participants would be more apt to avoid the negative effects of moral credentialing. For example, if participants would be asked to imagine themselves volunteering three hours a week at a homeless shelter during the first phase, then maybe they would be more likely to pledge money to benefit the homeless in the second phase. Thus, caring for the homeless in the first phase might "prime" caring for the homeless in the second phase.

An experiment conducted by Benoit Monin and Dale Miller at Princeton University suggests this does not occur in the way we might think.[16] Presumably, the influence of moral credentialing is more powerful than the benefits of such priming. In Monin and Miller's research, participants still manifested the negative effects of moral credentialing even though they were dealing with the same issue, that of sexual bias, in both phases of the experiment. The possible benefits of priming did not occur.

During the first phase of this experiment, participants reported their levels of agreement or disagreement with five statements about women. For half of the participants, the statements were always worded with an obvious bias to indicate something about "most" women. For the other half of participants, the statements were always worded with little or no bias. The statements simply indicated something about "some" women. Here are two examples for each condition:

High Bias Statements:
Most women are better off at home taking care of the children.
The best job for most women is something like cook, nurse, or teacher.

Little or No Bias Statements:
Some women are better off at home taking care of the children.

The best job for some women is something like cook, nurse, or teacher.[17]

Monin and Miller believed that participants in the high bias condition would strongly disagree with the statements. In doing so, the researchers predicted that these participants would start to "feel that they had stronger [moral] credentials as nonsexists." Such credentialing may or may not provide a kind of licensing to respond in a sexist way during a subsequent task. Monin and Miller did not believe participants in the little or no bias condition would experience the same degree of moral credentialing, since their statements were not extreme or controversial.

During the second phase, all participants were asked a series of questions that were not sexist in nature. But then they were asked to respond to a hiring situation at a cement manufacturing company. Here is part of the situation:

> Imagine that you are the manager of a small (45-person) cement manufacturing company based in [your state]. Last year was a particularly good one, and after you invested in increasing the output capacity of your plant, you decide that it would be very fruitful if you could find clients in other states to increase your business.
>
> ... You decide to appoint someone to go around to prospective clients to negotiate contracts.
>
> ... [You understand that if the person you choose] does not exude confidence in their technical skills [they] would not be taken seriously by potential clients. Realizing how useful such help would be for you, you decide to give the person chosen one of the top-five salaries in your company. Do you feel that this job is better suited for one gender rather than the other?[18]

Participants provided their responses to this hiring situation via 7-point scales ranging from "this is clearly a job for a woman" to "this is clearly a job for a man." The mid-point represents a non-sexist response.

Results indicated that participants who had the opportunity to disagree with obvious sexist statements during the first phase, those in the high bias condition, now tended to manifest higher amounts of sexist behavior in the second phase. They were more likely to report that this job at a cement manufacturing company might be best for a man, compared to the participants who did not have the earlier opportunity to disagree with obvious sexist statements.

Monin and Miller argue that the opportunity to challenge sexist statements allowed participants to establish enough moral credentials, at least for the moment, so they could be rather careless in a subsequent situation. Thus, moral credentialing and licensing can indeed show up even when we are dealing with the same moral issue (in this case sexism) in both the credentialing phase and the subsequent test phase. In a follow-up experiment, Monin and Miller also demonstrated that "participants who had established credentials as nonprejudiced persons revealed a greater willingness to express a politically incorrect [prejudicial] opinion."[19]

A Consideration

As mentioned, I volunteer with a homeless shelter program during the winter months in Pennsylvania. Occasionally I promote this endeavor. In doing so, I often encourage people to increase their levels of care and concern for people who are less fortunate. But is it fair for me to suggest that other people increase their care and concern for something I care about?

Probably not. I am succumbing to the psychological kind of *cornucopian myth*. If there is a limit to what people can genuinely care for, then perhaps I am asking too much. It is likely that these other people already care about a variety of important things. If they do as I suggest and increase their care and concern for those who are homeless, especially to the degree I suggest, it will probably create a strain on their psychological *caring capacity*. To be fair, perhaps I should warn them of this possibility. Or, I should help them identify where their increased caring should come from. In other words, what is it in their lives that they should care less about?

Chapter 11

Unconscious Processing: It's Superior

"Clearly, the adaptive unconscious can outperform consciousness
at every turn. Why, then, do we even have conscious processing,
if it is only a stupider and slower way of doing the same things
[as unconscious processing]?"
– Roy Baumeister, "The Unconscious is Alive and Well"

Throughout this book I have highlighted the importance of the unconscious level of awareness. It affects how we perceive and respond to other people. And it contributes to our inability to understand ourselves very well. But I am guessing some of you are still thinking, "Okay . . . unconscious processing has some influence, but it's minimal at best." In this chapter, consider the possibility that not only is it important, but in many ways it is the superior level for processing information. It is the level that initiates most of what we do and often produces the best results.

Remember the picture depicted in Figure 11.1 (introduced in Figure 2.1)? Conscious processing is represented with one thick wavy line. One line because it has very limited capacity, thick because it is a noticeable kind of processing, and wavy because it is effortful and slower. Unconscious processing is represented by multiple dashed lines. Multiple lines because it allows us to deal with a lot of information at one time, and dashed because it occurs very fast. Presumably, its ability to deal with information is about 200,000 times greater than that of conscious processing.[1]

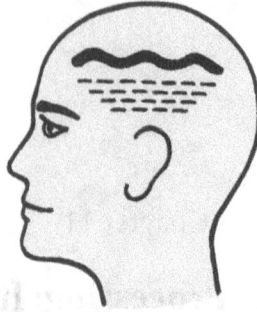

Figure 11.1: Two Levels of Processing

Thus, there are clear reasons to believe that what goes on unconsciously might be superior to what goes on consciously. But it is only now that researchers are making the case more adamantly. In doing so, they almost always start by referring to classic research conducted by Benjamin Libet in the 1980s.[2]

Which comes first, the things we do or our conscious awareness for the things we do? We usually think that it is conscious awareness that comes first. Then our actions come second. But Libet showed the opposite. He had research participants move one of their fingers to a specific environmental cue. He assumed that before such a response could occur, a certain region in the brain would need to be activated. This is the so-called "action potential" described in most General Psychology textbooks.[3] Using sophisticated equipment, he was able to measure the amount of time that occurred between this neural activity and the behavioral response. It averaged about one-half second.

Where does conscious awareness fit in? Most people would predict that conscious processing precedes the specific neural activity that causes the action, suggesting that consciousness is in control of the action. Instead, Libet found that the conscious experience occurred after the specific neural activity that caused the finger to move, but before the actual finger movement. Thus, something other than conscious processing must be serving as the initial cause for the neural activity and the subsequent movement. Libet and many others say it is unconscious processing that is activated by environmental cues.

As Tor Norretranders suggests, this should be obvious. In *The User Il-*

lusion: Cutting Consciousness Down to Size, Norretranders says that "unless consciousness just hovers freely in the air, it must be linked to processes in the brain." Of course. And these processes "must necessarily start up before consciousness appears."[4]

The most thorough argument for the superiority of unconscious processing has been put forth by Daniel Wegner in *The Illusion of Conscious Control.* It's provocative. Wegner says, "We do things, and when we do them, we experience the action in such a way that it seems to flow seamlessly from our consciousness. We feel that we cause ourselves to behave."[5] But this is an illusion! It only feels like conscious processing is initiating and guiding our behavior. Then Wegner goes on to say,

> The real causal sequence underlying human behavior involves a massively complicated set of mechanisms. Everything that psychology studies can come into play to predict and explain even the most innocuous wink of an eye. Each of our actions is really the culmination of an intricate set of physical and mental processes... However, we don't see [all] this. Instead, we readily accept a far easier explanation of our behavior: We intended to do it, so we did it.[6]

Or, as the novelist Thomas Wolfe summed up metaphorically, "Let's say you pick up a rock and you throw it. And in midflight, you give that rock consciousness and a rational mind. That little rock will think it has free will and will give you a highly rational account of why it has decided to take the route it's taking."[7]

Two questions. First, if conscious processing is in charge of our mental lives the way we usually think, then why is it sometimes hard to control or change our own thoughts? For example, did you ever experience a time when it seemed almost impossible to get an unwanted thought out of your conscious mind? If consciousness is the starting place for thoughts and behaviors, and if indeed it is in control, then this should be very easy to do.

Second, occasionally when a person is dealing with a complex issue or has an important decision to make, someone else suggests they should "sleep on it." Why would "sleeping on it" do any good? Unless sleeping somehow minimizes what consciousness contributes to the decision-making process and in turn, maximizes what unconscious processing might contribute. Presumably, whatever it is that unconscious processing might contribute can be very important.

There are a variety of experiments that have been conducted to suggest that what goes on unconsciously is superior to what goes on consciously. And there are three ways in which it happens. First, our conscious experience often has trouble predicting future behavior, suggesting it is overrated and not in control as much as we think. Second, there are clear demonstrations that unconscious processes often come first. Perhaps they always come first. Third, when put to the test, unconscious processing can outperform conscious processing in interesting ways. Now consider six experiments that are supportive.

Conscious Processing is Overrated

The first two experiments demonstrate that conscious processing, while good, is not as effective as it's cracked-up to be. In turn, this opens the door for unconscious processing to show its superiority. Both experiments were conducted by Nicholas Epley and David Dunning at Cornell University.[8] These researchers used a series of experiments to demonstrate that people are not very good at predicting their own behavior. If indeed conscious processing is as effective as we usually believe, and if indeed it controls behavior, then it should have a good feel for what it is going to do. Consciousness should be very good at predicting its own behavior.

At Cornell University, there's an annual tradition called "Daffodil Days." It's a four day event where students and faculty purchase daffodils to raise money for the American Cancer Society – a worthwhile endeavor. In one experiment, Epley and Dunning surveyed students about one month before "Daffodil Days." They asked the students if they would purchase a daffodil during the upcoming event and how many they believed they would purchase. A very high percentage of the students, 83%, reported consciously that they would purchase at least one flower, and on average, each student predicted they would purchase two. But during "Daffodil Days," only 43% of these students actually purchased a flower, and on average each student purchased only 1.2 flowers. Their conscious predictions were about half correct.

In a second experiment, Epley and Dunning evaluated the degree to which participants could accurately predict how much money they might donate to a charity organization, if given the chance. Again, this is an opportunity for consciousness to predict its own future behavior. Participants were paid $5.00 to take part in this research. During the first phase, all participants completed a lengthy questionnaire that lasted about 20 minutes. Unbeknownst to the participants, the specific questions were not related to the research.

At the end of the questionnaire, one group of participants was given $5.00 each for their participation along with an envelope that contained a packet of information to read and consider. The information was about three charity organizations – *The Salvation Army, The American Red Cross, and The Society for the Prevention of Cruelty to Animals.* These participants were informed that if they wanted, they could donate some of their payment to one of these charities. To do so, they simply needed to place the money in the envelope, identify the charity that should receive it, and seal the envelope.

A second group of participants was also given $5.00 each for responding to the initial questionnaire. And they were given the same packet of information about the three charities. However, this group was not given the opportunity to actually donate money to one of the charities. Instead, they were asked to hypothetically consider what they would do, if they were given the opportunity to donate money. They were asked to write how much money they would donate and to which charity it should go. So how much money do you think this group of participants "predicted" they would give, on average per person?

The second group of participants predicted, consciously, that they would donate $2.44 out of the $5.00, on average per person. But the first group of participants, who actually had the opportunity to donate money, averaged donating only $1.53 per person, a little over half the amount the other group predicted. Assuming both groups were fairly equivalent on all other factors related to charitable giving (which is what we do when we randomly assign participants to groups), then this study also shows that we tend to be lousy predictors of our own behavior.

Unconscious Processes Occur First

The next two experiments demonstrate how unconscious processing apparently precedes conscious processing, just as Benjamin Libet demonstrated in his finger-moving research. So perhaps unconscious processing is the starting place for all of what we do.

A few years ago, there was a controversy in a city in Italy over the possible expansion of a United States military base. The city was Vicenza in northern Italy, and the controversy received a lot of attention in the local media. Silvia Galdi and several colleagues conducted an experiment to investigate what residents of Vicenza believed, consciously and unconsciously, about this divisive issue. [9]

First, Galdi and colleagues asked each participant to complete a survey with various questions about the possible expansion of the military base. Thus, participants reported their beliefs consciously. In doing so, a fair number of participants indicated that they were "undecided." Were they? Or, is it possible that they were actually decided, unconsciously, but did not realize it, consciously?

Second, each participant completed a version of the Implicit Association Test (IAT) as described in chapter 3. Specifically, they performed the Single-Category IAT, similar to the short paper-and pencil version depicted in Figures 5.2 and 5.3. Using a computer, they needed to categorize as fast as they could, pictures of the military base with either positive words or negative words. Results indicated that many of the participants who reported that they were undecided about the military expansion issue, consciously, indeed expressed a preference unconsciously. It appears the *undecided* participants were actually *decided*, albeit unconsciously.

At a later time, the researchers asked each participant to again respond to a survey to evaluate how they might vote on this issue, if given the chance. Results indicated that participants who reported that they were consciously undecided in the initial survey now had a preference, and their preference was almost always consistent with what they manifested during the IAT. Galdi and colleagues conclude that "decision-makers sometimes have already made up their mind at an unconscious level, even when they consciously indicate that they are still undecided."[10]

A similar experience occurred for me a few years ago, although not nearly as important or newsworthy. Nearing the end of a U.S. college football season, one of the teams that play in the same conference as my alma mater Penn State was about to compete in a major New Year's Day bowl game. The team is one that Penn State fans consider to be a rival and almost always despise. I remember thinking consciously, that I must root for this rival team when it plays its opponent, because if it wins, then that will make Penn State and all teams in the conference look better.

When that bowl game started, I consciously cheered for that rival team for about five minutes. Then very quickly, I realized that there was no way I could root for this team, consciously or unconsciously. In hindsight, I am convinced that my unconscious knew all along that I could never favor this rival team no matter who they competed against in a bowl game. Consciousness only caught on to that fact after the game had started.

A different experiment, but with a similar message, was conducted by Robin Tanner and several colleagues at Duke University.[11] This experiment clearly demonstrates that what goes on unconsciously can initiate behavior, even when we are convinced that it was a conscious choice that did so. It also shows that it is the environment that often comes first and activates the unconscious processing. But of course, consciousness will take credit for what just happened.

In separate sessions, Tanner and colleagues gave each of their participants an opportunity to observe a confederate (a helper of the researchers) talk about an upcoming advertisement for television. The participants believed the confederate was simply another participant, as themselves. They were told to watch and listen to the confederate and remember as much information as they could from the descriptions of advertisements that were presented. As the confederate presented information, he or she also munched on one of two different snacks – either animal crackers or goldfish crackers, available in separate bowls.

Conveniently, the real participants also had separate bowls available in front of them, and yes the bowls contained animal crackers and goldfish crackers. So the real participants had the same opportunity to munch on the very same type of snack. Which snack the confederate ate was randomly determined for each participant. Results indicated that participants tended to munch on precisely the same snack the confederate was munching on. Thus, they mimicked the behavior of the confederate.

Then during a second and ostensibly unrelated phase, all participants responded to a survey about different snacks – 30 different snacks to be exact, with animal crackers and goldfish crackers among the possibilities. The participants who mimicked the choice of the confederate in the first phase, tended to give higher ratings of liking for the specific snack they munched on, compared to the alternative. And when asked, they tended to say that their higher ratings were based on their own pre-existing preference for the corresponding snack. It appears that they never realized that their choice in snack and corresponding ratings were influenced by the confederate in the first phase.

Brian Nosek, Anthony Greenwald, and Mahzarin Banaji provide a summary for all these kinds of studies:

> Among earthly organisms, humans have a unique propensity to introspect or look inward into the contents of their own minds, and to share those observations with others. With the ability to introspect comes the palpable feeling of "knowing," of being objective or certain, of being mentally in control of one's thoughts, aware of the causes of one's thoughts, feelings, and actions, and of making decisions deliberately and rationally. Among the noteworthy discoveries of the 20th century was a challenge posed to the assumption of rationality. [In a variety of studies], psychologists have shown the frailties of the minds of their species.[12]

Unconscious Processing is Best

The final two experiments demonstrate how what goes on unconsciously can actually produce superior outcomes compared to what goes on consciously. In both experiments, some participants would have opportunities to spend extra time focusing conscious processing to deliberate over an upcoming decision, while other participants would not have such opportunities. Instead, they would spend extra time relying on unconscious processing, independent of conscious influence or interference. In the end, which kind of extra processing will lead to the best decision?

Ap Dijksterhuis and Zeger van Olden asked students at the University of Amsterdam to make decisions about visual art.[13] Participants were asked to evaluate five artistic posters and eventually choose one for their own apartment or dormitory. The posters were presented digitally via computer. Three were abstract paintings and two were photographs.

At the beginning of the experiment, each participant was given a chance to see each poster, one at a time for 15 seconds each. Then during an intermediate phase, one group of participants, the *conscious processing (along with unconscious processing) group,* was asked to carefully analyze each poster, one at a time for 90 seconds each, and write what they liked and disliked about each poster. Thus, these students used 7.5 minutes of focused conscious processing to form opinions about each poster. Such processing may or may not help when it comes to making a quality decision. Presumably unconscious processing was also engaged for the 7.5 minutes. (Note: 5 posters X 90 seconds each = 7.5 minutes.)

Another group of participants, the *independent unconscious processing group* was not given the opportunity to use extra conscious processing in the intermediate phase. Instead they were asked to perform an unrelated thought-provoking task, solving various anagrams for 7.5 minutes. So these participants could not continue evaluating the posters consciously. But given the huge capacity for unconscious processing, they were still able to use some of that capacity to continue processing information about the posters, unconsciously, and independent of what conscious processing was now dealing with.

At the end of the experiment, all participants in both groups were given a final chance to see the five posters. The posters were presented simultaneously, and the participants rated how much they liked each one. Then as the participants left the experiment, they were asked to choose one of the posters as a gift, something they could display in their apartment or dormitory. They tended to pick the one they rated the highest.

About four weeks later, the researchers called all the participants, as many as they could based on availability. They asked each participant how satisfied they were with the poster they chose. Interestingly, the participants who used *independent unconscious processing* to further evaluate the posters during the intermediate phase, reported higher satisfaction with their posters, compared to those participants who used additional *conscious processing.* Furthermore, the participants in that *independent unconscious processing group* stated that they would want more money for their posters, if asked to sell the posters, compared to those in the *conscious processing group.*

These results clearly support the idea that something about unconscious processing, if it occurs while consciousness is distracted with another task, can indeed be superior to what might go on with extra conscious processing – at least superior when it comes to our own subjective preference for something in life. In explaining their results, Dijksterhuis and van Olden propose that conscious processing is relatively narrow. It cannot focus attention on too many things at one time. It almost always overlooks something that might be important in any given situation. Unconscious processing is not limited in this way. So it has an important advantage, and if it can spend some time dealing with information on its own without conscious meddling so to speak, it can lead to superior outcomes.

Timothy Wilson and Jonathan Schooler conducted a similar experiment with students at the University of Washington.[14] This experiment demonstrates that not only can unconscious processing be superior when forming subjective, personal preferences (like preferences for visual art), but it can also be better for producing results that match what so-called experts think about a certain choice.

Wilson and Schooler set up a taste-test – a "Jam Taste-Test." Using information provided in *Consumer Reports*, they picked five different brands of strawberry jams or preserves. They picked the jams ranked 1st, 11th, 24th, 32nd, and 44th, based on overall evaluations from seven taste-test experts. Then each participant had an opportunity to taste and evaluate each jam.

As they tasted the strawberry jams, half of the participants were given an extra opportunity to consciously (and unconsciously) analyze their affinity for each jam. They were instructed to write their reasons for liking or disliking each jam. The other half of the participants were not given this extra opportunity to consciously analyze each jam. Instead, they were told to analyze why they chose their major field of study, and they were instructed to write their reasons for doing so. Thus, the first group of participants used more *focused conscious processing* in evaluating the jams. For the second group, it was assumed that while they focused on writing about why they chose their major, a fair amount of *unconscious processing could continue evaluating information* about the jams independent of conscious influence.

Results showed that the evaluations of participants in the second group, the ones who used *independent unconscious processing*, came closer to matching the rankings of the so-called experts. Again, something about what goes on unconsciously while consciousness is distracted, seems to be particularly beneficial and superior to what extra conscious processing might contribute.

In the "evaluating art" experiment, Dijksterhuis and van Olden suggested that consciousness tends to overlook information that could be potentially useful, because it is so limited in what it can deal with at any given time.[15] Wilson and Schooler go further. In their "taste-test" research, they say that consciousness also tends to use its limited capacity in ways that are not very productive. It might focus too much attention on the specific task (something about the process), instead of focusing attention on the objects that need to be evaluated. As part of a later investigation, Schooler summed it up this way: "When you start becoming reflective about the process, it undermines your ability. You lose the flow" – the advantage of what unconscious processing can do on its own.[16]

The "flow" as Schooler suggests, might be the primary advantage of the adaptive unconscious. As Malcolm Gladwell says, it "crunches all the data it can from the experiences we've had, the people we've met, the lessons we've learned, the books we've read, the movies we've seen and so on, and it forms an opinion."[17] And that opinion can be better than anything consciousness comes up with when it is focused on a task. Dijksterhuis and van Olden use some creative imagery in describing how our unconscious minds can easily spread out its resources in many directions seeking to find whatever information it can that could possibly be useful. In doing so, Dijksterhuis and van Olden say it searches "the dark and dusty nooks and crannies of the mind."[18]

In sum, John Bargh concludes that a long time ago "Galileo removed the earth from its privileged position at the center of the universe." Now today, researchers are toppling consciousness from its privileged position as the superior level of cognitive processing.[19]

Chapter 12

Final Thoughts

"We are pawns in a game whose forces we largely fail to comprehend.
We usually think of ourselves as sitting in the driver's seat,
with ultimate control over the decisions we make and the directions
our life takes; but, alas, this perception has more to do with our desires
– with how we want to view ourselves – than with reality."
– Dan Ariely, *Predictably Irrational*

At this point, I hope all of us have a better understanding of the complexity of who we are. I hope too, the understanding comes with an increased sense of humility. Perhaps we are good – just not to the degree that we usually think.

Much of our misunderstanding is based on the discrepancy that occurs between what is conscious and what is unconscious. Several researchers propose that what is unconscious represents the truth of who we are. Consciousness simply represents who we want to be or how we want to be perceived.[1]

But if the unconscious part of our minds is so important, and in some ways superior, then why haven't we realized this before? Except for our friend from Vienna, Sigmund Freud, and his diehards, it has usually been rather "fashionable to view the unconscious as a relatively stupid system," as stated by Ap Dijksterhuis.[2] There are two reasons. First, and foremost, it is "UN-conscious." By definition, it is hidden. It is below the surface of conscious awareness, so how could we possibly know all of what goes on there? Second, consciousness by itself feels important and meaningful enough. Why would we even consider the possibility that there's something else going on that contributes to what we do in life?

In "The Unseen Mind," Timothy Wilson and Yoav Bar-Anan share a story to illustrate how the virtues of the unconscious tend to get overlooked.[3] During a trip to the west coast, one of these researchers, along with a spouse, was traveling on a scenic highway along the Pacific Ocean. They saw a sign indicating that elephant seals could be observed on the beach at an upcoming observation point. They decided to pull over at the next opportunity and check-it-out, to see what could be seen. They observed "five gigantic seals sunbathing on the beach." With that experience, they felt very satisfied. It seemed important and rich enough. So they eventually left that location.

It was only later that these two people realized there was much more to be seen. At a different observation point, "there were hundreds of seals sleeping, playing, and snuggling" on the beach and coastal area. This more important and richer experience could easily have been missed, because the first experience, by itself, was very meaningful and fulfilling. So it is with the human mind. As Wilson and Bar-Anan summarize, "When it comes to human introspection, there is no overlook from which one can see the vast contents of the adaptive unconscious. We are left with the illusion that the few 'elephant seals' we can see – the feelings and thoughts that are conscious – are the entirety of our mental life."[4] That illusion, by itself, seems important, rich, and meaningful enough.

The Two Levels Together

Today, several researchers are emphasizing how consciousness and unconsciousness must be considered as a team.[5] They each have their own virtues, and they are compatible. Which one is superior depends on what it is that we need to do. But again, cutting-edge research suggests it is the opposite of what we might expect. Some studies have indicated that when it comes to performing rather basic and straightforward tasks, conscious processing is superior and will yield the best results. But for more complex tasks with various nuances and intricacies, unconscious processing is superior and will yield the best results (as described in chapter 11).

To get a feel for this, consider finding the square root of a large number. As Dijksterhuis says,

Much evidence has been described implying that the unconscious can be very smart, but when asked, 'What is the
square root of 625?' your unconscious is not going to solve
it. You could be given a [conscious-consuming] distrac-
tor task lasting for months, but this question can only be
answered (assuming no calculator is used) after conscious
work. Likewise, consciousness is neither always smart (as
the current work shows) nor always slow (it finds the square
root of 625 in seconds). The bottom line is that both systems
can be fast, slow, smart, or stupid. It all depends on what
they are asked to do.[6]

For complex tasks (those that involve various nuances and intricacies),
keep in mind that it is the unconscious level that can deal with a lot of information at one time, and do so very quickly. Here's the summary Malcolm
Gladwell presents in *Blink: The Power of Thinking Without Thinking*:

When should we trust our instincts, and when should we
consciously think things through? Well, here is a partial
answer. On straightforward choices, deliberate analysis is
best. When questions of analysis and personal choice start
to get complicated – when we have to juggle many different variables – then our unconscious thought processes may
be superior. Now, I realize that this is exactly contrary to
conventional wisdom. We typically regard our snap judgment as best on immediate trivial questions. Is that person
attractive? Do I want that candy bar? But [recent research]
is suggesting the opposite: that maybe that big computer in
our brain that handles our unconscious is at its best when it
has to juggle many competing variables.[7]

This is basically the same as what Sigmund Freud proposed almost a
century ago: "When making a decision of minor importance, I have always
found it advantageous to consider all the pros and cons. In vital matters
however . . . the decision should come from the unconscious, from somewhere within ourselves."[8]

But while there are studies to suggest consciousness is best for basic tasks and unconscious processing is best for complex tasks, there are researchers who disagree. Although, those who disagree still believe that what goes on unconsciously is much more important than we usually realize. In an article entitled, "Think, Blink, or Sleep on It," Ben Newell and colleagues conclude that we should always be "cautious in accepting the advice to 'stop thinking' about complex decisions."[9]

Indeed, there's never a simple answer. Research in psychology will continue on.

Conclusion

Understanding the importance of the unconscious is a great first step to understanding ourselves and probably to becoming better people. Most likely, it also increases the chances that we extend the benefit of the doubt when evaluating others.

There are three additional ways we can get a better inkling of who we are. First, observe other people. Get a feel for what a typical person is like and what a typical person might do in certain situations. In doing so, we will have obtained a better understanding of ourselves and what we would do in the same situations. As Johann Wolfgang von Goethe once stated, "Self-knowledge comes from knowing other [people]."[10]

Second, notice how acquaintances, other than best friends, behave around us, and listen to what they say. This too, can provide useful information. For example, if they appear rather shy around us, there's a good chance we are not as friendly as we might think. And if they talk about us, there's a decent chance that what they say can be trusted. After all, they have a more objective view of us than we do ourselves. In some ways, they understand us better than we understand ourselves.

Finally, the third way we can better understand ourselves is by learning more about psychology and what is considered normative behavior for certain situations. Research can be very trustworthy, and it can provide a legitimate window into understanding ourselves. In chapter 11, I described research in which some participants had opportunities to predict how much money they might donate to a charity, and others had actual opportunities to donate money to the charities. Results suggested that people tend to only donate a little more than half of what they predict they will donate.

At an invited lecture at HACC: Central Pennsylvania's Community College, I described this research along with similar studies related to goodness. Then I suggested we could all have a better understanding of ourselves if we did this: "Take a moment to imagine how good you are. Also, think about what you might do within the next few weeks to manifest that goodness. Now cut those amounts in half, and you are probably closer to the truth."[11] If we are not as good as we think we are, at least we are probably half as good as we think we are.

References and Notes

Chapter 1: Exaggerations Abound

1. Alfred W. Adler, c.1900, see Calvin S. Hall and Gardner Lindzey, *Introduction to Theories of Personality* (New York: Wiley & Sons, 1985).
2. David G. Myers, *Exploring Psychology*, 5th Ed. (New York: Worth Publishers, 2002), 449-450.
3. Thomas Kida, *Don't Believe Everything You Think: The 6 Basic Mistakes We Make in Thinking* (Amherst, NY: Prometheus Books, 2006), 109.
4. Jonathan A. White and S. Plous, "Self-Enhancement and Social Responsibility," *Journal of Applied Social Psychology* 25, no.15 (1995): 1297-1318.
5. David G. Myers, *Intuition: Its Powers and Perils* (New Haven, CT: Yale University Press, 2002), 96.
6. Alf Boore Kanten and Karl Halvor Teigen, "Better Than Average and Better With Time: Relative Evaluations of Self and Others in the Past, Present, and Future," *European Journal of Social Psychology* 38, no.2 (2008): 343-353.
7. Joe Willie Namath, *I Can't Wait Until Tomorrow . . . 'Cause I Get Better-Looking Every Day* (New York: Random House, 1969).
8. Elanor F. Williams and Thomas Gilovich, "Do People Really Believe They are Above Average?" *Journal of Experimental Social Psychology* 44, no.4 (2008): 1121-1128.
9. Scott T. Allison, David M. Messick, and George R. Goethals, "On Being Better but Not Smarter than Others: The Muhammad Ali Effect," *Social Cognition* 7, no.3 (1989): 275-295, and Paul A.M. Van Lange and Constantine Sedikides, "Being More Honest but Not Necessarily More Intelligent than Others: Generality and Explanations for the Muhammad Ali Effect," *European Journal of Social Psychology* 28, no.4 (1998): 675-680.
10. Mohammed Ali, *The Greatest: My Own Story* (New York: Random House, 1975).

11. Van Lange and Sedikides, "Being More Honest but Not Necessarily More Intelligent," 676.

12. Ibid., 675-680.

13. Ibid., 675-680.

14. For Buddha, see the *Dhammapada*, verse 252. For Jesus, see the *Bible*, Matthew 7, verses 3-5.

15. Myers, *Exploring Psychology*, 449.

16. Kida, *Don't Believe Everything You Think*, 109.

17. Leonard Mlodinow, *Subliminal: How Your Unconscious Mind Rules Your Behavior* (New York: Pantheon Books, 2012), 200.

Chapter 2: More Complex Than We Realize

1. Benjamin Franklin, c.1750, quoted in Myers, *Exploring Psychology*, 8.

2. Jay L. Wenger and Richard A. Carlson, "Cognitive Sequence Knowledge: What is Learned?" *Journal of Experimental Psychology: Learning, Memory, and Cognition* 22, no.3 (1996): 599-619. Also see *Dual-Process Theories in Social Psychology*, ed. Shelly Chaiken and Yaacov Trope (New York: Guilford Press, 1999).

3. John A. Bargh and Tanya L. Chartrand, "The Unbearable Automaticity of Being," *American Psychologist* 54, no.7 (1999): 476.

4. Daniel Kahneman, *Thinking, Fast and Slow* (New York: Farrar, Straus, & Giroux, 2011), 4.

5. For Sigmund Freud's estimate, see Inna Burdein, Milton Lodge, and Charles Tabor, "Experiments on the Automaticity of Political Beliefs and Attitudes," *Political Psychology* 27, no.3 (2006): 359. For the current estimate, see Ap Dijksterhuis and Loran F. Nordgren, "A Theory of Unconscious Thought," *Perspectives on Psychological Science* 1, no.2 (2006): 95-109.

6. Timothy Wilson, *Strangers to Ourselves: Discovering the Adaptive Unconscious* (Cambridge, MA: Belknap Press of Harvard University, 2002), 105 and 102.

7. See Wilhelm Hofmann, Tobias Gschwendner, and Manfred Schmitt, "On Implicit-Explicit Consistency: The Moderating Role of Individual Differences in Awareness and Adjustment," *European Journal of Personality* 19, no.1 (2005): 25-49.

8. See Wilson, *Strangers to Ourselves*, and Ap Dijksterhuis, "Think Different: The Merits of Unconscious Thought in Preference Development and Deci-

sion Making," *Journal of Personality and Social Psychology* 87, no.5 (2004): 586-598.

9. Malcolm Gladwell, Blink: *The Power of Thinking Without Thinking* (New York, NY: Back Bay Books/Little Brown Company, 2005), 11-12.

10. Wilson, *Strangers to Ourselves*, 24.

11. See John R. Anderson, "Automaticity and the ACT-Super(*) Theory," *American Journal of Psychology* 105, no.2 (1992): 165-180, and Allan M. Collins and Elizabeth F. Loftus, "A Spreading-Activation Theory of Semantic Processing," *Psychological Review* 82, no.6 (1975): 407-428.

12. See B.R.Hergenhahn, *An Introduction to Theories of Learning* (Englewood Cliffs, NJ: Prentice Hall, 1988), 159-199.

13. Collins and Loftus, "A Spreading-Activation Theory of Semantic Processing," 407-428.

14. David E. Meyer and Roger W. Schvaneveldt, "Meaning, Memory Structure, and Mental Processes," *Science* 192, no.4234 (1976): 27-33.

15. Donald A. Norman, *The Psychology of Everyday Things* (New York: Basic Books, 1988), 115.

16. See Anthony G. Greenwald, Mahzarin R. Banaji, Laurie A. Rudman, Shelly D. Farnham, Brian A. Novak, and Deborah S. Mellott, "A Unified Theory of Implicit Attitudes, Stereotypes, Self-Esteem, and Self-Concept," *Psychological Review* 109, no.1 (2002): 3-25, and John A. Bargh, Mark Chen, and Lara Burrows, "Automaticity of Social Behavior: Direct Effects of Trait Construct and Stereotype Activation on Action," *Journal of Personality and Social Psychology* 71, no.2 (1996): 230-244.

17. See Wilson, *Strangers to Ourselves*.

18. Jonathan Haidt, *The Righteous Mind: Why Good People are Divided over Politics and Religion* (New York: Pantheon Books, 2012), 46.

Chapter 3: Do We Really Know What We Believe?

1. See Irene V. Blair, "Implicit Stereotypes and Prejudice," in *Cognitive Social Psychology: Princeton Symposium on the Legacy and Future of Social Psychology*, ed. Gordon B. Moskowitz (Mahwah, NJ: Lawrence Erlbaum, 2001), 359-374, and Markus Brauer, Wolfgang Wasel, and Paula Niedenthal, "Implicit and Explicit Components of Prejudice," *Review of General Psychology* 4, no.1 (2000): 79-101.

2. Fyodor Dostoyevsky, c.1870, available at https://implicit.harvard.edu/im-

plicit/demo/ background/psottestinfo.html (accessed May 2010).

3. Anthony G. Greenwald, Debbie E. McGee, and Jordan L.K. Schwartz, "Measuring Individual Differences in Implicit Cognition: The Implicit Association Test," *Journal of Personality and Social Psychology* 74, no.6 (1998): 1464-1480. Also see Greenwald, Banaji, Rudman, Farnham, Novak, and Mellott, "A Unified Theory of Implicit Attitudes, Stereotypes, Self-Esteem, and Self-Concept," 3-25.

4. Greenwald, McGee, and Schwartz, "Measuring Individual Differences in Implicit Cognition," 1479.

5. Ibid., 1464-1480.

6. Mahzarin Banaji, quoted in Beth Potier, "Prejudice is Not Just Black and White," *Harvard University Gazette,* April 18, 2002, available at http://news. harvard.edu/gazette/2002/04.18/03-banaji.html (accessed May 30, 2012).

7. A description of this *King of the Hill* episode is available at http://www. tv.com/king-of-the-hill/racist-dawg/episode/242650/summary.html (accessed June 2010).

8. For the paper-and-pencil IAT, see Brian S. Lowery, Curtis Hardin, and Stacey Sinclair, "Social Influence Effects on Automatic Racial Prejudice," *Journal of Personality and Social Psychology* 81, no.5 (2001): 842-855. For the items used in this evaluation of self-concept, see Laurie A. Rudman, Anthony G. Greenwald, and Debbie E. McGhee, "Implicit Self-Concept and Evaluative Gender Stereotypes: Self and Ingroup Share Desirable Traits," *Personality and Social Psychology Bulletin* 27, no.9 (2001): 1177.

9. Greenwald, Banaji, Rudman, Farnham, Novak, and Mellott, "A Unified Theory of Implicit Attitudes, Stereotypes, Self-Esteem, and Self-Concept," 3-25.

Chapter 4: Unconscious Content: It Matters

1. John A. Bargh, "The Cognitive Monster," in *Dual Process Theories in Social Psychology*, ed. Shelly Chaiken and Yaacov Trope (New York: Guilford Press, 1999), 361-382.

2. Patricia G. Devine, "Stereotypes and Prejudice: Their Automatic and Controlled Components," *Journal of Personality and Social Psychology* 56, no.1 (1989): 5-18.

3. Bargh, Chen, and Burrows, "Automaticity of Social Behavior," 230-244.

4. Ibid., 230-244.

5. Ibid., 230-244.

6. Lawrence E. Williams and John A. Bargh, "Experiencing Physical Warmth Promotes Interpersonal Warmth," *Science* 322, no.5901 (2008): 606-607.

7. Ap Dijksterhuis and Ad Van Knippenberg, "The Relation Between Perception and Behavior or How to Win a Game of Trivial Pursuit," *Journal of Personality and Social Psychology* 74, no.4 (1998): 865-877.

8. Ibid., 865.

9. Bargh and Chartrand, "The Unbearable Automaticity of Being," 468.

10. Russell H. Fazio, J.Richard Eiser, and Natalie J.Shook, "Attitude Formation through Exploration: Valence Asymmetries," *Journal of Personality and Social Psychology* 87, no.3 (2004): 293-311, and Aiden P. Gregg, Beate Seibt, and Mahzarin R. Banaji, "Easier Done than Undone: Asymmetry in the Malleability of Implicit Preferences," *Journal of Personality and Social Psychology* 90, no.1 (2006): 1-20.

11. Gordon D. Logan, "Toward an Instance Theory of Automatization," *Psychological Review* 95, no.4 (1988): 492-527.

12. John Gottman, *Why Marriages Succeed or Fail, and How to Make Yours Last* (New York: Simon and Schuster, 1995).

Chapter 5: Love the Sinner? Hate the Sin?

1. Jay L. Wenger, Kennedy N. Bota, and Peter Odera, "Evaluating Implicit Sentiments for Sinners and Sins: A Cross-Cultural Investigation," *International Journal of Psychological Studies* 4, no.2 (2012): 19-27.

2. Richard Beck, "Spiritual Pollution: The Dilemma of Sociomoral Disgust and the Ethic of Love," *Journal of Psychology and Theology* 34, no.1 (2006): 53.

3. Ibid., 53.

4. Greenwald, Banaji, Rudman, Farnham, Novak, and Mellott, "A Unified Theory of Implicit Attitudes, Stereotypes, Self-Esteem, and Self-Concept," 3-25.

5. Jay L. Wenger and Amy L. Daniels, "Who Distinguishes between Sinners and Sins at the Implicit Level of Awareness?" *The Journal of Social Psychology* 146, no.6 (2006): 657-669, and Wenger, Bota, and Odera, "Evaluating Implicit Sentiments," 19-27.

6. For the paper-and-pencil IAT, see Lowery, Hardin, and Sinclair, "Social Influence Effects on Automatic Racial Prejudice," 842-855. For a Single-Cat-

egory IAT, see Andrew Karpinski and Ross B. Steinman, "The Single Category Implicit Association Test as a Measure of Implicit Social Cognition," *Journal of Personality and Social Psychology* 91, no.1 (2006): 16-32.

7. Wenger, Bota, and Odera, "Evaluating Implicit Sentiments," 19-27.

Chapter 6: The Illusion of an Open Mind

1. Peter Wood, *A Bee in the Mouth: Anger in America Now* (New York: Encounter Books, 2006).

2. See Miles Hewstone, "The Ultimate Attribution Error: A Review of the Literature on Intergroup Causal Attribution," *European Journal of Social Psychology* 20, no.4 (1990): 311-335.

3. See Bargh, "The Cognitive Monster," 361-382, and David H. Ebenbach and Dacher Keltner, "Power, Emotion, and Judgmental Accuracy in Social Conflict: Motivating the Cognitive Miser," *Basic and Applied Social Psychology* 20, no.1 (1998): 7-21.

4. See Henri Tajfel, "Social Psychology of Intergroup Relations," *Annual Review of Psychology* 33 (1982): 1-39.

5. Jay L. Wenger, "Narrow-Mindedness among the Open-Minded," Unpublished manuscript, HACC: Central Pennsylvania's Community College, 2009.

6. Damian Stanley, Elizabeth Phelps, and Mahzarin Banaji, "The Neural Basis of Implicit Attitudes," *Current Directions in Psychological Science* 17, no.2 (2008): 164-170.

7. Jeffrey Kluger, "Race and the Brain," *Time* 172, no.14 (2008): 59.

8. Hewstone, "The Ultimate Attribution Error," 311-335.

9. Thomas F. Pettigrew, "The Ultimate Attribution Error: Extending Allport's Cognitive Analysis of Prejudice," *Personality and Social Psychology Bulletin* 4, no.4 (1979): 461-476.

10. Bargh, "The Cognitive Monster," 361.

11. Ibid., 362.

12. Wenger, "Narrow-Mindedness among the Open-Minded."

13. Ibid.

14. Bertrand Russell, c.1930, quoted in Gordon W. Allport, *The Nature of Prejudice* (Reading, MA: Addison Wesley Publishers, 1954), 19.

Chapter 7: I Am Right; You Are Wrong

1. Kathryn Schulz, *Being Wrong: Adventures in the Margin of Error* (New York, HarperCollins Publishers, 2010), 4.

2. Robert A. Burton, *On Being Certain: Believing You Are Right Even When You're Not* (New York: St. Martin's Press, 2008), xiii.

3. Ibid., 95. The "Hooray, I am right and I know it" statement was constructed by the author of this book.

4. Robert Abelson, "Beliefs Are Like Possessions," *Journal for the Theory of Social Psychology* 16 (1986): 222.

5. Schulz, *Being Wrong*, 103-104.

6. Drew Westen, Pavel S. Biagov, Keith Harenski, Clint Kilts, and Stephen Hamann, "Neural Bases of Motivated Reasoning: A fMRI Study of Emotional Constraints on Partisan Political Judgment in the 2004 U.S. Presidential Election," *Journal of Cognitive Neuroscience* 18, no.11 (2006): 1947-1958.

7. Ibid., 1947.

8. Haidt, *The Righteous Mind*, 88.

9. William James, *The Will to Believe: And Other Essays in Popular Philosophy* (New York: Longmans, Green, and Company, 1896).

10. See Burton, *On Being Certain*, and Haidt, *The Righteous Mind*.

11. Burton, *On Being Certain*, 103.

12. Schulz, *Being Wrong*, 107.

13. David G. Myers, *The American Paradox: Spiritual Hunger in an Age of Plenty* (New Haven, CT: Yale University Press, 2000), 285.

14. Kahneman, *Thinking, Fast and Slow*, 343.

15. See William J. McGuire, "Cognitive Consistency Theories," in *Encyclopedia of Psychology* Vol. 2, ed. Alan E. Kazdin (New York: Oxford University Press, 2000),139-140.

16. Dan Ariely, *Predictably Irrational: The Hidden Forces that Shape Our Decisions*, (New York: Harper Collins, 2008), 137-138.

17. Craig A. Anderson, Mark R. Lepper, and Lee Ross, "Perseverance of Social Theories: The Role of Explanation in the Persistence of Discredited Information," *Journal of Personality and Social Psychology* 39, no.6 (1980): 1037-1049.

18. Sigmund Freud, *Civilization and Its Discontents*, 1930, quoted in Myers,

Exploring Psychology, 298.

19. James A. Stoner, "Risky and Cautious Shifts in Group Discussions: The Influence of Widely Held Values," *Journal of Experimental Social Psychology* 4, no.4 (1968): 442-459.

20. Adapted from Robert A. Baron and Donn Byrne, *Social Psychology: Understanding Human Interaction* (Boston, MA: Allyn and Bacon Publishing, 1987), 395.

21. Markus Brauer, Charles M. Judd, and Melissa D. Gline, "The Effects of Repeated Expressions on Attitude Polarization during Group Discussions," *Journal of Personality and Social Psychology* 68, no.6 (1995): 1014-1029.

22. David Brooks, *The Social Animal: The Hidden Sources of Love, Character, and Achievement* (New York: Random House, 2011), 303.

23. Gary W. Heiman, *Basic Statistics for the Behavioral Sciences* Vol. 4 (Boston, MA: Houghton Mifflin Company, 2003).

24. Burton, *On Being Certain,* 220.

Chapter 8: Overvalued Values

1. Donnie Collins, "Top 10 Stories: No. 1, Jerry Sandusky Abuse Scandal," TheTimesTribune.Com, January 1, 2012, available at http://thetimes-tribune.com/sports/top-10-stories-no-1-jerry-sandusky-abuse-scandal-1.1251902#axzz1iEz91EUQ (accessed January 6, 2012).

2. Hugh Hartshorne and Mark A. May, *Studies in the Nature of Character, I: Studies in Deceit* (New York: Macmillan, 1928).

3. "NBA Rookie Camp Lesson No.1: Don't Smoke Dope at NBA Rookie Camp," *AOL News,* Sept 3, 2008, available at http://www.aolnews.com/2008/09/03/nba-rookie-camp-lesson-1-dont-smoke-dope-at-nba-rookie-camp (accessed January 28, 2012).

4. Max H. Brazerman and Ann E. Tenbrunsel, *Blind Spots: Why We Fail to Do What's Right and What to Do about It,* (Princeton, NJ: Princeton University Press, 2011), 68.

5. Janet K. Swim and Lauri L. Hyers, "Excuse Me – What Did You Just Say?!: Women's Public and Private Reactions to Sexist Remarks," *Journal of Experimental Social Psychology* 35, no.1, (1999): 68-88.

6. C. Greg Love and Jay L. Wenger, "The Architecture of Beliefs," research presented at the annual conference of the Southeastern Psychological Association, Atlanta, GA, March 2001.

7. Jay L. Wenger, "Implicit Components of Religious Beliefs," *Journal of Psychology and Christianity* 22, no.3 (2003): 223-229.

8. Nina Mazar, On Amir, and Dan Ariely, "The Dishonesty of Honest People: A Theory of Self-Concept Maintenance," *Journal of Marketing Research* 45, no.6, (2008): 633-644 .

9. Ariely, *Predictably Irrational*, 203.

10. Brazerman and Tenbrunsel, *Blind Spots*, 7.

11. John M. Darley and Daniel Batson, "From Jerusalem to Jericho: A Study of Situational and Dispositional Variables in Helping Behavior," *Journal of Personality and Social Psychology* 27, no.1 (1973): 100-108.

12. The "Parable of the Good Samaritan" is recorded in the *Bible, Matthew* 10, verses 25-37.

13. Peter M. Gollwitzer, Ute C. Bayer, and Kathleen C. McCulloch, "The Control of the Unwanted," in *The New Unconscious*, ed. Ran R. Hassin, James S. Uleman, and John A. Bargh (New York: Oxford University Press, 2005), 485-514.

Chapter 9: The Naïve Notion That "I Could Never Hurt Anyone"

1. Kurt Lewin, "Defining the 'Field at a Given Time,'" *Psychological Review* 50, no.3, (1943): 292–310.

2. Paul W. Andrews, "The Psychology of Social Chess and the Evolution of Attribution Mechanisms: Explaining the Fundamental Attribution Error," *Evolution and Human Behavior* 22, no.1, (2001): 11-29.

3. Stanley Milgram, *Obedience to Authority: An Experimental View* (London, England: Tavistock Publications, 1974). Also see Thomas Blass "The Milgram Paradigm after 35 Years: Some Things We Now Know about Obedience to Authority," *Journal of Applied Social Psychology* 29, no.5 (1999): 955–978.

4. "Adolf Eichmann," *Holocaust Encyclopedia*, United States Holocaust Memorial Museum, January 2011, available at http://www.ushmm.org/wlc/en/article.php?ModuleId=10007412 (accessed January 28, 2012).

5. In Milgram's original study, only about 2% of the participants quit the experiment at the very moment that they knew for sure that the actor-learner was experiencing pain. All other participants continued for at least some amount of time. See Milgram, *Obedience to Authority*.

6. Jerry M. Burger, "Replicating Milgram: Would People Still Obey Today?"

American Psychologist 64, no.1 (2009): 1-11. Also see Blass, "The Milgram Paradigm after 35 Years," 955-978. The countries include Australia, Austria, Germany, Italy, Jordan, South Africa, and Spain.

7. Thomas Blass, "From New Haven to Santa Clara: A Historical Perspective on the Milgram Obedience Experiments," *American Psychologist* 64, no.1 (2009): 37-45.

8. See Burger, "Replicating Milgram," 1-11, and Blass, "The Milgram Paradigm after 35 Years," 955-978.

9. See McGuire, "Cognitive Consistency Theories," 139-140.

10. Robert E. Knox and James A. Inkster, "Postdecision Dissonance at Post Time," *Journal of Personality and Social Psychology* 8, no.4 (1968): 319-323.

11. Eric Silver, "Bureaucracy, Loyalty, and Truth," *The PennStater* 99, no.3, (2012): 19-20.

Chapter 10: The Do-Gooder's Dilemma

1. See Benoit Monin and Dale T. Miller, "Moral Credentials and the Expression of Prejudice," *Journal of Personality and Social Psychology* 81, no.1 (2001): 33-43, and Sonya Sachdeva, Rumen Iliev, and Douglas L. Medin, "Sinning Saints and Saintly Sinners: The Paradox of Moral Self-Regulation," *Psychological Science* 20, no.4 (2009): 523-528.

2. See Roy F. Baumeister, "Ego Depletion and Self-Control Failure: An Energy Model of the Self's Executive Function," *Self and Identity* 1, no.2 (2002): 129-136, and James Y. Shah and Arie W. Kruglanski, "Priming Against Your Will: How Accessible Alternatives Affect Goal Pursuit," *Journal of Experimental Social Psychology* 38, no.4 (2002): 368-383.

3. William R. Catton, Jr., *Overshoot: The Ecological Basis of Revolutionary Change* (Champaign, IL: University of Illinois, 1982).

4. Baumeister, "Ego Depletion and Self-Control Failure," 129, and Kathleen D. Vohs, "Free Will is Costly: Action Control, Making Choices, Mental Time Travel, and Impression Management Use Precious Volitional Resources," in *Free Will and Consciousness: How Might They Work?* ed. Roy F. Baumeister, Alfred R. Mele, and Kathleen D. Vohs (New York: Oxford University Press, 2010), 67.

5. James Y. Shah, "The Automatic Pursuit and Management of Goals," *Current Directions in Psychological Science* 14, no.1 (2005): 12.

6. Monin and Miller, "Moral Credentials and the Expression of Prejudice,"

33-43, and Sachdeva, Iliev, and Medin, "Sinning Saints and Saintly Sinners," 523-528.

7. See Haidt, *The Righteous Mind*, and Arthur C. Brooks, *Who Really Cares? America's Charity Divide* (New York: Basic Books, 2006).

8. Brooks, *Who Really Cares?* 54.

9. Ronald J.Sider, *The Scandal of the Evangelical Conscience: Why are Christians Living Just Like the Rest of the World?* (Grand Rapids, MI: Baker Books, 2005).

10. Brooks, *Who Really Cares?*

11. Sachdeva, Iliev, and Medin, "Sinning Saints and Saintly Sinners," 524.

12. Angela J. Krumm and Alexandra F. Corning, "Who Believes Us When We Try to Conceal Our Prejudices? The Effectiveness of Moral Credentials with In-Groups versus Out-Groups," *The Journal of Social Psychology* 148, no.6 (2008): 689.

13. Sachdeva, Iliev, and Medin, "Sinning Saints and Saintly Sinners," 523-528.

14. Uzma Khan and Ravi Dhar, "Licensing Effect in Consumer Choice," *Journal of Marketing Research* 43 (May 2006): 259-266.

15. Ibid., 259.

16. Monin and Miller, "Moral Credentials and the Expression of Prejudice," 33-43.

17. Ibid., 35.

18. Ibid., 35.

19. Ibid., 33.

Chapter 11: Unconscious Processing: It's Superior

1. Dijksterhuis and Nordgren, "A Theory of Unconscious Thought," 95-109.

2. Benjamin Libet, "Unconscious Cerebral Initiative and the Role of Conscious Will in Voluntary Action," *Behavioral and Brain Sciences* 8, no.4 (1985): 529-566.

3. For examples, see Robert S. Feldman, *Essentials of UnderstandingPsychology*, 7th Ed. (Boston: MA, McGraw Hill, 2008), and Wayne Weiten, *Psychology: Themes and Variations*, 6th Ed. (Belmont, CA: Wadsworth/Thomson, 2005).

4. Tor Norretranders, *The User Illusion: Cutting Consciousness Down to Size* (New York: Penguin Press Science, 1998), 221-222.

5. Daniel M. Wegner, T*he Illusion of Conscious Will* (Cambridge, MA: Bradford Books, 2002), 2.

6. Ibid., 27.

7. Thomas K. Wolfe, presented in *I am Charlotte Simmons*, 2004, p. 283. It is quoted in Ap Dijksterhuis, Tanya L. Chartrand, and Henk Aarts, "Effects of Priming and Perception on Social Behavior and Goal Pursuit," in *Social Psychology and the Unconscious: The Automaticity of Higher Mental Processes*, ed. John A. Bargh (New York: Psychology Press, 2007), 51.

8. Nicholas Epley and David Dunning, "Feeling 'Holier Than Thou': Are Self-Serving Assessments Produced by Errors in Self- or Social Prediction," *Journal of Personality and Social Psychology* 79, no.6 (2000): 861-875.

9. Silvia Galdi, Luciano Arcuri, and Bertram Gawronski, "Automatic Mental Associations Predict Future Choices of Undecided Decision-Makers," *Science* 321 (August 2008): 1100-1102.

10. Ibid., 1101 and 1100.

11. Robin J. Tanner, Rosellina Ferraro, Tanya L. Chartrand, James R. Bettman, and Rick Van Baaren, "Of Chameleons and Consumption: The Impact of Mimicry on Choice and Preferences," *Journal of Consumer Research* 34, no.2 (2007): 754-766.

12. Brian A. Nosek, Anthony G. Greenwald, and Mahzarin R. Banaji, "The Implicit Association Test at Age 7: A Methodological and Conceptual Review," in *Social Psychology and the Unconscious: The Automaticity of Higher Mental Processes*, ed. John A. Bargh (New York: Psychology Press, 2007), 265.

13. Ap Dijksterhuis and Zeger van Olden, "On the Benefits of Thinking Unconsciously: Unconscious Thought Can Increase Post-Choice Satisfaction," *Journal of Experimental Social Psychology* 42, no.4 (2006): 627-631.

14. Timothy D. Wilson and Jonathan W. Schooler, "Thinking Too Much: Introspection Can Reduce the Quality of Preferences and Decisions," *Journal of Personality and Social Psychology* 60, no.2 (1991): 181-192.

15. Dijksterhuis and van Olden, "On the Benefits of Thinking Unconsciously," 627-631.

16. Jonathan W. Schooler, quoted in Gladwell, *Blink*, 122.

17. Gladwell, *Blink*, 85.

18. The "dark and dusty nooks and crannies" quote comes from Dijksterhuis and Nordgren, "A Theory of Unconscious Thought," 102.

19. John A. Bargh, "The Automaticity of Everyday Life," in *Advances in So-*

cial Cognition, Vol. 10, ed. Robert S. Wyer (Mahwah, NJ: Lawrence Erlbaum Associates, 1997), 52.

Chapter 12: Final Thoughts

1. See Wegner, *The Illusion of Conscious Will*, and Wilson, *Strangers to Ourselves*.
2. Dijksterhuis, "Think Different," 586.
3. Timothy D. Wilson and Yoav Bar-Anan, "The Unseen Mind," *Science* 321 (August 2008): 1046-1047.
4. Ibid., 1047.
5. See Dijksterhuis, "Think Different," 586-598, and Ben R. Newell, Kwan Yao Wong, Jeremy C.H. Cheung, and Tim Rakow, "Think, Blink, or Sleep on It? The Impact of Modes of Thought on Complex Decision Making," *The Quarterly Journal of Experimental Psychology* 62, no.4 (2008): 707-732.
6. Dijksterhuis, "Think Different," 597.
7. Gladwell, *Blink*, 267.
8. Sigmund Freud, c.1920, quoted in Dijksterhuis, "Think Different," 586.
9. Newell, Wong, Cheung, and Rakow, "Think, Blink, or Sleep on It?" 707.
10. Johann Wolfgang von Goethe, c.1800, available at http://www.famous-quotes.com/show/ 1026454 (accessed January 2012).
11. Jay L. Wenger, "A Modest Attempt at Understanding Ourselves," Honors Lecture presented at HACC: Central Pennsylvania's Community College, Lancaster Campus, October 13, 2011.

www.ingramcontent.com/pod-product-compliance
Lightning Source LLC
Chambersburg PA
CBHW052211270326
41931CB00011B/2307